HAPPY
on
PURPOSE

JENNIFER SPARKS

PRAISE for *HAPPY on PURPOSE*

"*Happy on Purpose* will change your life! Jennifer Sparks has written another fantastic book on how to live life more fully and more wisely. Changing perspective can change your life, and this book shows you how."

Cara Lockwood
USA Today Bestselling Author

"I am honored to have a first peek at *Happy on Purpose*, before it's rolled out to the masses. Jennifer, off a successful first book, *WFT to OMG: The Frazzled Female's Guide to Creating a Life You Love*, has done it again with a heart-felt yet tough love approach to being *Happy on Purpose*. Using her real-life experiences and proven tools for success, Jennifer practices what she preaches. She is a shining example of what being happy means, what being happy looks like and what being happy can accomplish. *Happy on Purpose* is a sure path to happiness!"

Shelly Drymon
Co-Founder The Rescue Yourself Project
www.pattyandshelly.com

"Jennifer hits the nail on the head with *Happy on Purpose*. She gives a step-by-step guide on how to create lasting happiness from the inside-out that works! Jennifer breaks down the process of how happy people think and act and proves that happiness is accessible to everyone and anyone, no matter what your current circumstance."

Mary Sabo
Life and Happiness Coach, RYT & Blogger
www.Mary-Sabo.com

Shastidy —
In each moment
be happy!
Jen ☺

STOKE Publishing
www.swiftkicklife.com

Dedication

Yo! Super awesome children of mine,
I love you to the moon and back.
As you enter the teen years and settle there, I am happy to report you get more marvelous with each moment. I know that some days you think I am seriously uncool, but I know that one day you are going to look back on this time in our lives together and laugh from your belly remembering all the jokes and goofy times. I mean, seriously? Frogger and Bean, you are going to change the world in your own beautiful ways. Thank you for being so smart, witty, and downright spectacular. You both appear to have been born with old souls and thoughtful minds. I cherish every minute of every day with you both.

This book is dedicated to anyone who hears that voice deep inside saying,
"I just want to be happy!"

ঌ৹৵৾

"Happiness comes from within. This is why, if you truly want to be happy, you need to work on yourself, first." ~ Dr. J. Mercola

ঌ৹৵৾

Yep, I had heard it a million times but what the heck did that *really* mean?

Start reading and find out!

Contents

Foreword

I was thrilled to recommend Jennifer's first literary effort, *WTF to OMG*, simply because it was, in fact, *that* terrific. Therefore, my mind was already happily prepared to write another review for this book because I knew that she would have absolutely stellar content the second time around. Apparently, I am either prophetic or simply a good judge of quality. I would like to think both actually. However, there is no denying that this book surpassed my expectations. We upgraded the review to the foreword because I have a few extra things to say.

We have two really big choices in life: live or die. If you are going to live, LIVE. If you don't, you might as well have chosen the latter. However, when all you are trying to do is survive, seeing life differently seems impossible. If life is throwing lemons at you at a rate of WTF, it is difficult to imagine being in a place where significant struggle is not a daily occurrence. Nonetheless, if we are going to make a happy life, we have to carve out small moments for happiness and make room for growth if we ever hope to turn those fragments of happiness into bigger, longer, more frequent moments. Don't let regret keep you stuck. This constant rumination will stunt your momentum and can prevent you from reaching out toward new things. I discuss this with my clients and patients who want a transformation but are confounded when I place the onus on them to make it happen. I have quite often heard, "well that is easier said than done." To which I reply, "and...?" I am really just a professional reminder. None of what I tell those I work with is novel information. This is all common **knowledge** but not common **practice**. Knowing is not enough. Shifts in perspective start with an informational download but taking actionable steps to put those thoughts to use is a non-negotiable cog in the wheel for shifting to occur. Do you want something? Do you want it more than you are afraid of it? What is your intention for your life? Decide and then do what you intended. My guess is that you have and it is why you have this book in your hands.

Happy on Purpose is a powerfully penned, first-person account that delivers more than wise advice or airy mantras for happiness. Jennifer knows first-hand what it is like to struggle and not just once or even a few times. Someone's struggle is unique to them -- it is not what we struggle with but the emotions from our struggles that form the common thread between each of us. Your experience is just that. There is no one exclusive kind of trauma that qualifies you to seek solace, knowledge or rebirth. But once you have been exposed to what's possible, happiness seeps in and it will compound itself exponentially. It's like rabbits in love: a few things can beget lots of little things! Then before you know it, there are big things and those spawn more things, big and little! It is truly a never-ending loop!

What has been seen cannot be unseen. Once you have experienced the 360 view from the top, you cannot help but to be changed and you will want to share your new experience with others! Happiness is not only an emotion; it's a way of life. It can't and shouldn't be contained. That is what Jennifer has done for us in this book. She shares herself as she unwinds her way from emotionally dark places to her purposeful awareness of existing light. The light is there for all of us and she helps us gain access to it. So many things Jennifer talks about in *Happy on Purpose* will resonate with you. You will be truly amazed. She learned to capture her moments, call out those identifiable feelings, and she has used it to thrive! You will raise your personal vibration higher, thus attracting others with energetic levels on par with yours. This will allow you to continue your trajectory into the life you are meant to truly live. You will read this and be stunned. You will refer back to *Happy on Purpose* more than once and recommend it to at least one other person who needs to hear these words.

Celebrate yourself for taking a step forward in your happiness! Don't be discouraged if you don't feel like dancing a jig right away. Let the messages sink in. Sure, there are times when things just suck. Two steps back after you just made a step forward? Don't fret! Where I come from we call that a cha-cha!

Happy reading!

Angelique F. Trigueros, M.S., CCC-SLP, CPC is a speech-language pathologist with almost 20 years in the health care field and is a Certified Professional Life Coach. She is working diligently on her doctoral dissertation in Health Psychology and intends to be Dr. Angelique by the end of 2015! She is sole proprietor of New Leaf Life Coaching, the Director of Mindset and Accountability Coaching for Michael Mapes, LLC and one third of the 3 Sassy Broads, a trio committed to the infusion of happiness through the transformation of self. Find Angelique online at: www.newleaf-lifecoaching.com and www.3SassyBroads.com.

Introduction:
YOU HAVE A CHOICE TO MAKE

My daughter and I were driving in the car one evening. The radio was playing quite loudly (hey, she's fifteen) and she was singing along. I began talking about something and she asked me to be quiet for a second because "her absolute favorite part of the song was coming up." I had been thinking about what brings people joy in ordinary days and in that moment, for her, it was a single note of her favorite song sung to perfection. For me, it was watching her experience that little sliver of simple joy because I knew how hard the previous few months had been for her. Nothing about this story is extraordinary. Yet I was paying attention to the simplicity of this moment and drinking in the details of it like a thirsty runner.

Have you ever really taken a moment to think about all the little things that could bring you joy in an average day if you were open to receiving and enjoying them? The amazing thing is that **these little slivers of joy happen anyway,** even if you are not paying attention. I have seen how the practice of happiness can transform the way people see their world and how they begin to see beauty in the most amazingly simple things. Have you ever stopped to contemplate how much joy slips by us as a result of our busy lives and our tendency to be focused on the future instead of in the moment?

I have.

You wouldn't recognize me if you'd met me ten years ago. That is an entirely different story, but for now, let's just say I was not a happy person and for the most part it wasn't even my fault. (I am being sarcastic because I am all about accepting responsibility for your own life.) My unhappiness showed in my health, my thoughts, my clothes and my food choices. It showed in the way I walked, my lack of eye contact, a tanking confidence level and in my desire to isolate myself from others. Unbeknownst to me, several of my old habits actually contributed to misery's grip on me. While it was my responsibility to be happy, I just didn't seem to think things could change. I was overweight, stressed out, unhappy, anxious, angry and seriously S.T.U.C.K in Unhappyland. And I was scared.

Fast forward a decade and for the most part, nothing has changed except my outlook on life. I changed my mindset, and I changed my behaviors to align with these new mindsets. Otherwise, I still have the same two kids. I am still divorced. I have the same job, the same house, the same van, and many of the same obligations and responsibilities. I was always rushing as fast as I could to the next thing because I operated on the belief that as soon as I put some things (or stressors) behind me, I would find happiness just waiting eagerly for me to claim what was rightfully mine. After all, hard work creates happiness, doesn't it?

I often heard myself saying things like, "As soon as I get this done, I will be happier." Or, "If only I didn't have to deal with this, my life would be amazing." With this belief system firmly in charge of my actions, I worked VERY hard to achieve things because I truly believed this would result in my happiness. When that system didn't work as I had planned I just worked harder. Still the ground beneath me disappeared and I was knocked on my ass where misery pinned me into a place of stagnation and fear paralyzed me. Eventually, I had my *WTF Moment* and was inspired to change my life. (You can read about that entire journey and the tools I used to overhaul my life in my bestselling book, *WTF to OMG: The Frazzled Female's Guide to Creating a Life You Love*. This is a great book for the person who has no idea where to start!)

These days, I think taking a moment to just absorb and enjoy what's happening around me regardless of my to-do list or high stress events is one of my most effective mechanisms for dealing with stress ... and I have plenty of it, just as you do. One thing that has changed is I've embraced simple new habits that allow my focus to be on things that bring me joy and make me happy. I've learned to look for these things even on the bad days. I have a very low tolerance for bullshit. If I find myself around it, I remove myself from it. I have learned how to sort through all the incoming stimuli and pick the items worth focusing on. I make a conscious effort to practice happiness and you can too. **Being *Happy on Purpose* is NOT about having the perfect life, it is about learning how to be happy by using your focus to define your experiences.**

What I am going to model for you in this book is HOW, despite the shittiest of days, I decided to be *Happy on Purpose* and how I go about that process. I am not a guru or a superstar. I am just a single mom trying to do better and live better. I know the practice of happiness can change your life, because it changed mine dramatically. While I don't go into the nitty gritty details, like many of you I have had my share of ups and downs. Sometimes the downs were severe. Life can change in a second and I experienced that first hand. Divorce. Single parenting. A sick child. Car accidents. Aging parents. How can we create a buffer that allows us to take care of ourselves while we take care of others without crumbling into an exhausted, miserable mess?

Truly, it is about the little things and taking notice of the abundance you have surrounding you. I know, I can already hear some of you telling me you have nothing in your life that makes you happy right now but hear me out. **This isn't about what is in your life and the happiness these things may bring. It is about what is in your head and the actions you take as a result of your thoughts.**

Let me put it this way, whether you choose to notice the abundance that surrounds you or not, it is still there. Right now, you might not be able to see any of it because of the way you have trained your brain to deal with your environment but it is still there. If this abundance is truly there, and you train your mind to learn how to see it, things really do get better. And they can get better fast. The best part? It's free! These habits that make up your happiness practice enable you to put things into perspective (both good and bad). **Your actions make the ultimate difference in how things turn out**. This is really what deciding to be happy is all about: your perspective and your understanding.

I invite you to visit my website, www.swiftkicklife.com to download the free companion resource I created to make my suggestions more action based. (Download details to follow- keep reading.) **After all, until your behavior changes all things will remain the same.** And, if I am not mistaken, you are reading this book because you are ready for that change. You are ready to be ... *Happy on Purpose!*

How This Book Works

Happy people do things differently. They have this ability to hone in on what brings them happiness even if external events are negative and begging for their attention. They sift through what happens around them and they focus on the things that fuel their happiness. I can't say for sure how they come to possess these skills and habits, but I do know that even people who don't have these skills can learn them because I did just that. In this book, I will provide examples of how I applied what I am sharing with you to circumstances in my own life to further illustrate what I mean. Happiness is absolutely your choice. These examples will model the process of making the choice to move towards happiness even when life's circumstances are not ideal.

❧

"Happiness is rarely absent; it is we that know not of its presence."
~ Maurice Maeterlinck

❧

My purpose for sharing personal stories with you is to show how simple it can be to shift your focus to the things that bring you joy, and away from the things that frustrate, anger, depress or stress you. Consequently, this shift in your focus and perspective impacts how you feel. **Being *Happy on Purpose* is** about making a conscious decision in each moment to move towards or away from happiness. It is not about a perfect life. It is not about having things. It is about creating YOUR experience and being open to the beauty, joy and abundance that already exists in your life and calibrating yourself to recognize it with ease.

This book can be your guide to happiness. Consider for a moment if we twist the common idea that we should pursue happiness then remodel it to incorporate the idea that happiness can be cleverly crafted and created by each of us.

∽≪

"Happiness cannot be traveled to, owned, earned, worn, or consumed. Happiness is the spiritual experience of living every minute with love, grace, and gratitude." ~ Denis Waitley

∽≪

After reading this book you will:

- Understand why you need to **accept responsibility** for creating your own happiness
- Understand that **happiness is a learned way** of thinking and acting
- Understand how to use your **mindset** and align your **actions** to cultivate happiness

- Personally **define what happiness means to you,** and **understand the nature** of happiness so you can build self-confidence and resilience for difficult times
- Become familiar with the **things that happy people do differently,** and have the opportunity to begin integrating these practices (tools) into your own life so you can upgrade your happiness and life satisfaction.

The HappyPack
Companion Resource

As I mentioned earlier, I designed a free HAPPYPACK that compliments this book. Make sure you grab your copy at www.swiftkicklife.com. You will need to enter your email address to access the free download and then watch for a confirmation email. If you do NOT get it, check that naughty SPAM or JUNK folder! Once you confirm your email, you will receive a second email with a link to grab the *HAPPYPACK!* You will need to use CODE: HOP2014 to unlock the download page!

Anyone who knows me knows I am all about action. In my first book, *WTF to OMG*, I offered tools and strategies to help people make changes in their lives. I also offered a free downloadable Companion Journal so readers had the structure and support they needed to begin making changes right away.

My books are not books you simply read, they are books you DO. Why?
We can sit around all day talking about the changes we need to make to upgrade our lives but the simple fact remains that nothing changes unless something moves and that something must be YOU! Action creates movement, change and new opportunities. It opens doors. It changes lives. It is where the success happens.

In *Happy on Purpose*, I give you some happiness habits to begin implementing into your life. My greatest fear is that you will set this book aside and forget its message and that the suggestions will not become practice. This is why I designed The HAPPYPACK. You have nothing to lose!

Are you in?

Here. We. Go!

"I know for sure that what we dwell on is who we become."
~ Oprah Winfrey

PART 1:
Can I Really Learn to Be Happy?

What erroneous beliefs might you have about happiness and do they hold you captive in a place of dissatisfaction or misery? Creating happiness in your life can only happen if you are alert, aware and prepared to change your mind and your behavior. But first, you have to believe your mindset matters and your behaviors and actions can propel you to new levels of happiness.

જ⊷≪

"I freed a thousand slaves. I could have freed a thousand more if only they knew they were slaves." ~ Unknown

જ⊷≪

In this first section of *Happy on Purpose*, we are going to get this big, white elephant of a question out of the room. Yep, we are going to dig in and push it right out to the front step, trunk and all. I know it's in here. I can hear it breathing. You know it is too because it is the first question that came to your mind, right?

Can I really learn to be happy?
My purpose in this section is to make you a believer. I know this might be a difficult task because you may have picked up this book as a last resort. You may have tried everything else already. You may be at your wit's end. You may be facing what

seems like insurmountable obstacles and happiness may seem like a very distant dream. You may think I am full of absolute crap. I totally get that. I remember how I felt when I couldn't think about anything other than getting through the day and then some twit would get in my face and tell me I needed to be more positive. How the hell was I supposed to do that? It is my goal to make you believe, that despite where you may be right now, happiness is possible.

I ask for your patience as I explain the entire process and provide some tangible and relatable examples because as T. Harv Eker says, "the most dangerous words are 'I know this already.'"

You very well may have heard some of what I am about to share with you, but if my perspective can put a new spin on it for you, it might be what makes the difference. I am going to tell you how I learned I could be happy and then how I actually DID it. This is my journey, and yours may play out differently. I am sure you realize that knowledge alone does not create the change we seek, it is the behavior based on that knowledge that does. Information does not create transformation; integration, action and application of that information is what changes lives.

While I have spent endless hours trying to make sense of my own experiences, I have also done a tremendous number of online courses and spent hours researching happiness and positive psychology because it truly fascinates me. I was always curious about how some people could rise above and thrive in lives that continually tested them, yet others struggled with lives that seemed, by all means, easy and carefree. I am *that* girl who reads self-development, research, psychology and coaching books every chance she gets. While this might make me a nerd, it also means you can learn from what I have learned and lived. Even better, the time spent on the pursuit of knowledge, allows me to connect actual research to my own personal journey, which has helped me understand what I managed to do through trial and error (read that as "trial and error and error and error"). This also allows me to share with you the best pieces of my journey and to give you BS free examples of what exactly I mean, how I transformed my own mindset and behaviors, and strengthen the examples with actual research.

This isn't a cabbage soup diet.
Positive psychology is a legitimate field of scientific study that focuses on exploring the strengths and virtues that enable individuals to thrive. While some of the findings can create results fairly quickly, there is no magic pill or quick fix for increasing your happiness if you aren't the one doing the work for yourself. Being *Happy on Purpose* is all about using your mindset to cultivate and nourish the life you always dreamed of having. Only YOU know what that feels like and how brave you are going to have to be to achieve it.

All I can tell you is that the journey is worth it. The effort is worth it. Happiness is worth it.

Chapter 1:
LEARNED HAPPINESS

Having been quite unhappy for a number of years, it seemed almost silly for someone to suggest that if I actually wanted to be happier I just had to *learn* how to be happier. Actually, truth be told, it pissed me off! A lot. It implied that being unhappy had been my choice all along because I hadn't bothered to *learn* how to be happy. It seemed like a trite suggestion, like learning to tie my shoes was all I needed to do and bliss would be mine. But here is the thing: learning to be happy is about changing your mindsets and then aligning your behaviors with these new mindsets. It was true and if I wanted to learn to be happy, I needed some new skills.

The problem was, I didn't know learning to be happy was something I could actually do. I always thought of happiness as just a *feeling*. "I am feeling sad" or "I am feeling happy" were things I heard myself say. I never heard myself say, "I am think-ing sad or thinking happy." I never told myself to act happy or act sad. I just *felt* that way. When I first began to realize the path to happiness was not through my feelings but through the way I thought and acted, which directly impacted my feelings, I suddenly saw where I could make drastic improvements in my life. I believed that my environment and life had changed and THAT is what brought the unhappiness. I was a victim of circumstance. I think it is clear that this erroneous belief was my first problem. It's not easy to learn you are your own problem, but I was. I needed to get out of my own way and I was miserable enough to try anything.

Somehow, I had to come to understand that if I changed the way I thought, I could change the way I acted (or didn't,) and then suddenly other things would begin to change. It made perfect sense because everything is connected. If you change one thing, other things have to respond. Furthermore, I hadn't even considered that because my level of happiness radiated from me towards others, it truly would impact all parts of my life. If you can increase your happiness, you can give yourself a major life makeover.

I also had a question. I had been happy once, did this mean I had unlearned or forgotten how to be happy? I didn't think so! I don't ride my bike every year but I still know *how* to ride it when I jump on!

However, if I was going to be absolutely honest (and since that is the entire point of this book) I think that under tremendous stress, I forgot some of the daily habits that made me a happy person in the first place. I became disengaged and in my lack of awareness, I wasn't really making conscious choices anymore and I was allowing life to happen TO me. (I was tired, overwhelmed, disengaged and passive.)

I had stopped practicing being happy. I had forgotten, at some point along the way, that it feels good to focus on the good. Instead, I started to complain about everything that was wrong and I took on the role of a victim. When I became the victim in my own life, I gave up 100 percent of my power to circumstance. If I had no control, I couldn't change it, right? For ten years I fluctuated between being unhappy and disengaged to being unhappy and frustrated.

I knew something had to change but had no real idea what that something was. Perhaps you feel the same way right now?

According to University of California researcher, Sonja Lyubomirsky, "40 percent of our capacity for happiness is within our power to change." She claims that 50 percent is determined by our genetic makeup and about ten percent is due to circumstance. (Not the 100 percent I claimed it to be!) In *The Myths of Happiness*, she shares scientific evidence that it is our mindset, not our circumstance that matters most!

40 freaking percent?

Imagine if right now, you were 40 percent happier. What would that mean for you? How differently might you feel? If you were 40 percent happier, how might that impact your relationships, your job, your outlook on life, your immune system, your energy, your eating and movement habits, your enjoyment on a day-to-day basis, and dare I even say it, your life span?

I know it sounds crazy! But if you are unhappy right now, consider the impact that a 40 percent improvement plan could have on your life! You should be squirming in your seat right now with newly found hope! Imagine the possibilities that could open up for you in your own life with such a drastic increase in your happiness level!

കൈൽ

"Happiness doesn't depend on any external conditions; it is governed by our mental attitude." ~ Dale Carnegie

കൈൽ

Through the practice of happiness habits, everyone can learn to enhance their life and satisfaction. In our modern world, many of us have been conditioned by this idea that we need to chase happiness. We think the new car, the new job, the degree or the new relationship is going to bring us happiness and fulfillment. If we think and believe that, then happiness is out of our control, isn't it? Happiness becomes totally dependent on external forces. What happens once we get all that stuff? We want more or different stuff. We work harder. We aren't happy until we get it, but then, we want more again.

I remember telling myself all the time, "As soon as we get this or that, things will be so much better or easier." I bought into that way of thinking for a long time and I worked very hard to make things happen, but the happiness never arrived. I told myself again, "Well as soon as I do this or that, I will be happy." Nope, degrees didn't make me happier and neither did other achievements. In fact, looking back now I realize (and can finally admit) nothing really would have made me happy because I was chasing a moving target. There would always be something else to work towards, a new goal or another award, but what about right now? Could I learn to be happy right now, where I was, with what I had, in this life, because now is all I had for certain?

Living in the uncertain future, leaning on the "as soon as I get the next greatest thing" mentality doesn't bring happiness anymore than the arrival of whatever achievement or luxury item you have been waiting for. You must be happy first.

As Joel Osteen puts it, "You can be happy where you are." You can learn to be happy now, with the life you live, with what you have and you can be happy AS you move towards a goal rather than only when you arrive there.

Furthermore, once you upgrade your happiness, amazing things begin to happen. Drama matters less. Complaining means nothing because it doesn't serve you, and you can easily identify it and quickly disengage. It is easier to let things go that cause you pain or distress because you have a better sense of what feels "good." You stop judging. You get better and better at choosing happiness. The good in your life multiplies because of your energy. Every facet and domain of your life begins to change. The more control you gain over your happiness, the more powerful you become. **Understanding your happiness comes from within you when you accept responsibility for your thoughts and actions is the key to the happiness puzzle.**

჻

"Be at least as interested in what goes on inside you as what happens outside. If you get the inside right, the outside will fall into place." ~ Eckhart Tolle

჻

The purpose of this book is to teach you what habits you can integrate into your life today so you can GET HAPPY NOW! Open up your heart and your mind. It's already in you. *Happy on Purpose* will simply teach you to see it and once you do, your life will change forever.

Chapter 2:
HAPPINESS IS A SKILL SET

I will suggest that finding happiness is an individual approach to living your life, but as we move through this book, you will be asked to define happiness for yourself. So please, understand that what I share here is merely a suggestion to get you thinking and moving towards a definition that works for you. Imagine looking through a kaleidoscope at all the beautiful patterns. A slight turn of the kaleidoscope barrel and a stunning new picture can appear. Colours change, patterns develop and new shapes appear. Some of these designs you will love, while others you will not. It doesn't matter because you can simply turn the barrel again. Life is just like that. There are so many variables at play and the designs change quickly. To fully understand what details you love the most, it might be easiest to change only one variable at a time. When you get to the section on behaviors to consider implementing into your life, I will suggest you take one or two that seem meaningful and realistic to you. Start there. Keep notes. Reflect and revise. Pay attention to what you love about it (or don't) so you can keep what works for you and toss the rest!

Happiness comes as a byproduct of discovering your life's purpose and moving towards goals that are important to you while paying close attention to the daily behaviors you practice. This refines your focus on things that bring you pleasure, joy and contentment. While arriving at the destination and achieving your goals is a rewarding experience, the journey needs to be joyous and rewarding as well. When you are aligned from the head down with your thinking, your heart follows. Amazing things begin to happen. You become happier.

Some have asked me if people really need to learn these things. Some people do seem to know more intuitively how to create happiness. Some people may have known at one point and lost their way. I have often thought about how trauma and life experiences can change belief systems and trigger different thought patterns, which result in different actions. Therefore, my answer is not necessarily that they need to learn these things but they need to be aware of these habits and how they can impact their lives. Ultimately, the rest is up to them.

People need to understand what is happening when they struggle to achieve happiness. They need to understand why staying comfortable can shortchange you in the long run. They need to understand what forces are at play and how they might be playing a role in their overall unhappiness and how they can use opposing forces to lift them out of despair. As I said earlier, some people have an intuitive understanding of what it takes to be happy and others, well ... they don't. However, the good news is that research has shown that happiness can be learned just like helplessness can be learned. If Sonja Lyubomirsky is correct about 40 percent of our happiness being up to us, I think that suggests that the practice of happiness it is a skill worth learning!

I Just Want to Be Happy

Have you ever heard yourself say, "I just want to be happy?" Just like playing the piano, very few of us sit down and tickle the ivories perfectly the first time. But we understand with practice, we can achieve what we never thought possible the first time we played. We can keep raising the bar as we learn new things. We begin to see what is possible. I believe the same goes for happiness. Practice the skill set that increases your happiness and before you know it, you have reprogrammed your automatic responses (thoughts, behaviors and habits) and you can raise the bar again.

Train Your Brain

Increasing your happiness level is really a game about where you assign your focus. We only have so much attention; we need to spend it wisely on things that matter to us and things that will increase our happiness. **We need to use focus to lift ourselves up, not to bring more stress and turmoil into our lives.** I must confess that I never watch the news. My reasoning is simple: negative, catastrophic events come at you faster than you can deflect them. I can sense my anxiety level increasing when I watch negative news story after negative news story. Can I control any of the events that are being reported to me? No, I can't. I can always go looking for details about an event if I need it. After all, Google is just a click away. So, instead of allowing my focus to be spent on the negative, and what I can't control, I train my brain to help *sort my environmental influences to decrease my stress and increase my bliss.*

I remember when I was eagerly awaiting my engagement: all that was on my mind was getting engaged. I was focused on all things wedding related. It seemed like everywhere I went, my eyes dropped to left hands to check for rings! It seemed like everyone had become engaged overnight. Then, when I was married and trying to conceive, pregnancy was all I could think about, and all I could see were pregnant bellies. When my daughter was diagnosed with Epilepsy, suddenly I saw references to this disorder all around me. And I noticed for the first time how often people crack jokes about it. Same for divorce. Once that became my reality, I could identify divorced people all over the place. I could even watch people eating in restaurants and identify those who were unhappy because I had become hyper sensitive to this experience. My brain was trained to see certain things based on my experiences and focus.

In my first book, *WTF to OMG*, I talked about the power of visualization and explained how the subconscious mind doesn't know the difference between a real and an imagined experience. Because of this, you can use visualization to train your brain (on a subconscious level) to obtain things that may seem unreachable otherwise. Personally speaking, when I put things on my vision board, I am training myself what to see in my environment. I am training my brain to *zoom in* on only the things that will serve my goals, and to let the other stuff slip by me. For example, if I put a trip to Europe on my board, I begin to notice amazing deals and possible European packages everywhere. Or, if I put an athletic achievement on my vision board, I communicate to my subconscious that I am interested in things that will help me reach this goal so my brain is on alert for them. Suddenly, I become more aware to opportunities I need so that I can learn more about how I can make that athletic goal a reality (races, special coaches, training camps or workshops). My environment hasn't changed. My exposure to opportunities hasn't changed. **My awareness has.** If I am interested in that training objective and I see an advertisement for a training camp, I am far less likely to notice or pay attention to the pub-crawl poster next to it because partying wasn't on my vision board but the athletic achievement was. My brain has to pick what matters over what doesn't. I prefer it attends to what matters to me.

Because your beautiful mind can only have so much information in it at a given time, if you take the proactive step of training your brain to look for what you need, it begins to filter out the stuff that doesn't matter. Instead it alerts you to the things that you have told your brain you want to know about. Visualization, focus and meditation can all impact your brain's preliminary sorting mechanism. If you set your brain up right, it is like installing a few useful SPAM filters on your brain's email. It will filter some of the noise and clutter in your environment and direct you towards what is good for you! When you open your brain's inbox there will be ten worthy emails sitting there for you instead of hundreds of useless messages that you then have to waste your energy sorting. I might add, having highly-tuned filters also significantly reduces your stress level because then you just stop dealing with the stuff that doesn't matter to you. **You can train your brain to see what you seek.**

Chapter 3:
WHAT CAN I DO TO BE HAPPY?

Breathe.
Be open to new ideas.
Breathe again.

❧

"I am determined to be cheerful and happy, in whatever situation I may be; for I have also learned from experience that the greater part of our happiness or misery depends upon our dispositions, and not upon our circumstances." ~ Martha Washington

❧

Some people truly don't believe we are "supposed to be happy" and they never buck the status quo to actively create their own happiness because of this belief system. People like this will continue to toil away in dead-end jobs, and suffer through shitty relationships feeling totally unfulfilled because "no one said life was supposed to be easy." Or they would stay in a situation that was personally unfulfilling because they feel totally obligated to someone or something else, even at the cost of destroying themselves.

Unfortunately, this can impact you as you begin making changes to create your own happiness, so be prepared. When you construct your own happiness, these non-believers may be watching and judging you. They might even get in your face to let you know they think you are crayyyzeee! "Who do you think you are to want these things?" "How the hell are you going to pay the bills being an 'artist'?" "Who told you life was supposed to be good or fair or happy?"

Understand they come from a different place and that their current belief systems are interfering with their understanding of happiness. Know it. Accept it. Create your happiness anyway.

Your Happiness Matters

I remember the struggle I had when my son was born. My former spouse and I were living in the United States while attending graduate school. I had a few social connections, but I didn't have any really close friends. My family and my social network were in Canada and I had already been worn down by my struggles with infertility.

As luck would have it, I finally did become pregnant. My pregnancy was difficult and morning sickness extended to include all day and all night. I become a pro at whipping out my plastic puke bags behind the wheel or in mid-step at the mall. At four months along, I defended my thesis with a mouthful of soda crackers and I left the room periodically to vomit into a garbage can I had thankfully placed in the hallway. That entire experience fell substantially short of glorious.

Eager to have a perfect birth story to make up for the rough pregnancy, I was devastated when the delivery became an emergency C-section. When I woke up from the surgery and my former spouse told me we had a son, I didn't believe him! I had no memory of the birth or much of the labour. I had also developed toxemia and was holding onto enormous amounts of fluid. My head was huge. My fingers were like little sausages. Trying to bend my legs was like trying to bend a hot dog in half. I met a lady in the elevator three days post C-section (as in the baby was out of me) and when she wished me good luck with my delivery, I let the elevator doors close behind her and then burst into tears. In addition to this sudden fluid gain, the C-section left me with limited use of my core and I was a mess. I couldn't even get in and out of bed myself and now I had this little person to take care of as well! I was sent home with my OBGYN's wife's cell number. While at the time I thought that was really kind of him, I think my OBGYN was maybe trying to derail what he knew was likely headed my way.

An emotional and mental shit storm was waiting for me. He knew it, and I was still trying to live out my dream of this ideal "pregnancy/delivery/new mom" scenario with my head firmly planted in the sand. I was very disappointed that I couldn't even get the whole pregnancy thing right, after all, isn't that the one thing women are supposed to be able to do?

Following the birth of my son, I was troubled with some serious postpartum depression and anxiety. I didn't even recognize it in myself, and it was my mother who mentioned it when she came to visit three weeks later. I ignored her. In hindsight, I couldn't even make a decision about what to eat and I was quite disabled by my thought processes. I then developed mastitis and had to stop nursing my son the moment my doctor made that diagnosis. I know now that in some strange way I was grieving the experience I wanted to have so badly, and was disappointed that I couldn't seem to get anything right.

I ended up in my OBGYN's office discussing treatment options for mastitis. He stopped mid- sentence and addressed my state of mind. He told me that if I was struggling around my son, that even as a baby, he would pick up on it and it could influence his development. I have never forgotten his warning. I listened, as tears streamed down my face, and I surrendered to him for help. Xanax, Ambien and Zoloft followed.

I hadn't slept for months because I had anxiety about endless irrational fears that came out of nowhere. That voice inside my head never shut up. It was on Speed. I have never felt more useless or messed up in all my life. Clearly, my happiness mattered to my family as well. It makes total sense now. I just couldn't see it at that time, because my thoughts seemed so scrambled.

I hated accepting the fact that maybe I needed help. I hated that what I wanted so badly had ended up messing up my head. I reluctantly took the medications and promised myself I would use them as a hand up and that I was going to take charge of getting better. If not for my own sake, I would certainly do it for my son. Remember, your happiness matters AND it can impact others as well.

A few foundational items here to consider:

1. **Put Yourself First**
   You need to understand putting yourself first is not selfish and you should not feel guilty about it. Why? Well in my example above, what if I had NOT put myself first and gone to the doctor to get help? Not only could mastitis have caused a serious health threat to me, but the depression and anxiety could have a serious impact on me, my spouse and my child. Your loved ones want you at your best. Strive to be your best and they will thank you. If they don't, there are other issues at play there.

2. **Look at the Big Picture**
   Try to think in terms of the big picture and don't get snagged on the little details that make you crazy. This is the same as "don't sweat the small stuff." Learn to see the bigger plan and how life events have lined up along the way to bring you where you currently are. Look for the lessons. When I stopped zeroing in on little incidences and was able to see a bigger plan, it made letting go of things that didn't serve the bigger plan much easier. This made me less bitter and more accepting of what came my way. For example, did it really matter that I didn't have the ideal birth story? No. I had a healthy son to be grateful for and that is really what mattered.

3. **Dream BIG**

   Get yourself some kickass dreams. ***Dreams are the lighter fluid and opportunity is the flame.*** If you don't have dreams when the flame comes by, nothing catches fire. And for goodness sake have some fun here! Dream big and don't worry about the 'how' of things. Once you decide you are going to move to a tropical location and work, your brain takes in the environmental stimuli in a different way. It seeks out the opportunities for you and starts laying them at your feet and suddenly it all seems like a big coincidence. This is where it gets scary good because all you have dreamed about starts happening and you can't believe it! Your job? DREAM BIG. Dream big, exciting, mind-messing, enormous dreams.

4. **Define What Makes You Rich**

   If you only consider money as a means to riches, I beg you to reconsider. I am rich because I have two great kids. I am rich because of the amazing friends and family I have in my life. I am rich because I have love. I am rich because I love to write and I am able to do it! I am rich because I see the value in experiences over things. Are you rich? List the ways.

5. **If You Want to Really Mess People Up - Be Happy**

   We all have been there when someone who is happy leaves a room and everyone looks at one another and someone cracks the joke about wanting what he or she smokes! Why is it so unusual to be happy? Why is it socially acceptable to be cranky? Why is it socially acceptable to brag about working twenty-hour days (and missing out on family things to do that)? But if you manage to balance your life fairly well, make time for yourself and create a happy life that isn't filled with "material possessions" people look at you sideways? They might even call you lazy or unmotivated! And all you are is happy!

6. **Happiness is About You**
   Happiness does not come from other people. If you are searching for the "one" person that makes you happy, look in the mirror. I remember a client telling me that she had a major breakthrough in terms of her relationships. She told me she had blurted out to her boyfriend, "I wouldn't be any less happy if you were not in my life. You are not my happiness, I am." When she realized her happiness was up to her alone, she let him go. She no longer attached being happy with being with him. She was hanging onto him because she thought if she lost him, she would lose her happiness. She told me she felt incredibly powerful when she realized her happiness was not dependent on him, because it made her understand she could be alone and still be happy.

7. **Change Your Outlook on Disappointments**
   If something doesn't work out, expect that something better is on the way. We all have dreams of things happening that will change our lives for the better and when something doesn't work out, we can be so emotionally attached to that event we lose hope. When

something doesn't happen for me and plans fall apart, I ask myself what might be coming instead. When shit really hits the fan and things seem bleak, instead of asking myself, "Why is this happening to me?" I ask myself, "Why is this happening FOR me?" What is it that I need to take away from this to improve my life? What is my lesson?

8. **Choose Your Words Carefully**
   Emotions are attached to words so if you use a string of profanity to describe your ex-spouse, expect that those words are going to drop little emotional grenades in *your* body. You speak shit. You feel shit. Express praise where possible and if you can't then hush up. Look for the happier parts of your world to speak about and clean up the emotionally charged words you use to elicit a more positive emotional response. **Ranting about something is like spewing negativity all over the place.** It's messy! It gets all over you and other people and impacts everything. Complaining about your "asshole" boss or that "stupid" professor or "idiot" store clerk doesn't change anything other than YOUR emotional well-being. I am so sensitive to people ranting that I have been known to hang up phones or walk away in mid-conversation just to stop the flow of ickiness! As Tony Robbins says, "Simply by changing your habitual vocabulary – the words you consistently use to describe the emotions in your life – you can instantly change how you think, feel and how you live."

ॐ∽

"The key to happiness is letting each situation be what it is instead of what you think it should be." ~ Mandy Hale

ॐ∽

Forces at Play

I remember vividly the day I heard someone say it is impossible to feel fear and gratitude in the same moment. I forget who said it but it got my attention. It was one of those moments when everything around you slows down and you feel like the sky has just opened up for you. Suddenly, I realized if I didn't want to feel the fear, I just had to focus on gratitude. It was like I was gifted with the easy button for moving past things in my life that held me back. Things that had caused me to continuously trip as I tried to move on suddenly became easier to move past. I had been living a fear-based life and it had paralyzed me!

If you pay attention and start looking you will find nothing but opposing forces, conditions, or directions surrounding you. Up and down. Left and right. Happy and sad. Fearful and grateful. Sick and healthy. Acceptance and resistance. Trust and doubt. Praise and criticism. Abundance and lack. Kindness and cruelty. Good and evil. Positive and Negative. Responsibility and blame.

Once I started looking, I saw these opposing forces everywhere! Then, I realized if choosing gratitude meant I couldn't choose fear then the same would apply for all of these other opposing forces or conditions. If I didn't want to experience lack, I focused on abundance. If I hated the way doubt made me feel, I opted for trust (and therefore, people I could trust). If I sought out the positive, the negative would matter less. Really? Yes! Really.

If, instead of resisting something, I asked myself, "What can I learn here?" I immediately shifted my focus to the numerous positive ways to look at the situation. If I can't forgive someone, it festers in ME, not them. I always think of this quote by Buddha when I think of the importance of forgiveness: "Holding onto anger is like drinking poison and expecting the other person to die." Understanding forgiveness was a gift I gave myself, not the person who'd hurt me was critical. I needed peace more than I needed to be angry. I have always said that you cannot put a price tag on your peace of mind. A sense of contentment and peace puts your body into a drastically different state. You can't let all the good in if you have your arms crossed and a scowl on your face.

When I was younger, everything seemed to be a bigger deal than it actually was. I reacted more strongly to events back then than I do now. My years of experience have taught me there is no sense getting my knickers in a knot about things I cannot change or things I cannot control. Ever wonder why grandparents don't rattle that easily? They. Have. Been. There. It almost makes me laugh how chill my father can be. If my teenage child crashes his car, the first thing on his mind is likely that his parents are going to kill him. The first thing on my mind? Is everyone okay? Did anyone get hurt? We have a different perspective.

Cars are things that can be replaced. And if you have really messed up and the car can't be replaced, there is always a bus. As long as no one was hurt, your life can be modified a bit (hello, bus pass) to keep you moving forward. Perhaps having a bus pass will teach valuable lessons about how stupidly expensive it is to have your own car anyway. Perhaps you will realize it is easier to get around by bus and train than having to try to find a parking spot. Maybe after six months with a bus pass, you will see how much extra cash you have for other things you love to do, like travel. The car accident ends up being a gift because it opens up an entirely new world for you with your extra cash flow. Maybe that car accident and the resulting bus pass allows you to understand early in life that just because everyone else has a car, doesn't mean you need to have one, especially if it prevents you from doing things you love. Maybe this realization sets you up on a life path where you begin to understand you don't need to play follow the leader because YOU are the leader of your own life!

My favorite of these opposing forces is responsibility and blame. This one seems to flip the world on its ass. If you stop blaming people for all that has gone wrong in your life, you have decided to choose responsibility. In doing so, the control belongs to you. Blaming others puts you into the victim mindset and like I mention in *WTF to OMG*, victim mindsets aren't going to take you any place you really want to go. Once you accept responsibility for every domain in your life - relationships, career, money, physical fitness, emotional well-being - and so on, your entire world changes.

Framing my world with opposing forces became a game. It's a tremendously fun AND rewarding game. Try it!

PART 2:
Defining Happiness and Understanding Its Nature

To feel fully alive you must walk through life awake. Likewise, to be happy you must define it for yourself and understand its nature so you can awaken to the happiness already within you.

In this section, we will attempt to address what happiness actually is and what it is not. There are a few things I know for sure about happiness, but then I also know what makes me happy isn't likely going to make you happy and vice versa. It's critical that people define happiness for themselves. If I passed you my happiness plan, you might do all the steps on my plan and STILL end up being unhappy simply because my plan is based on my definition of happiness.

That would really be disheartening if you did all this work to be happy, only to end up no further along. So hear this: define what happiness means to you. Be as specific as possible because specific details allow for a more specific plan. The more specific you are, the more time and effort you can save yourself as you begin the journey to Happyland. As I mentioned earlier, I had an epiphany when I realized that the *feeling* of happiness was a result of a combination of a mindset and behavior change that resulted in the feeling of happiness. You don't just "feel happy" something has to take you there.

Be on the alert for your own epiphanies! These are somewhat fleeting so have a pen and paper ready or be prepared to grab your phone and type a line of gibberish into your Notes app! If you have a flash of genius, write it down and then do your best to explain it to yourself before you forget it. I have often had these genius thoughts pop into my head only to float out almost as quickly, which is why I have notes everywhere. I equate it to when I find myself walking down the hallway towards the bedroom but forget what I am going there for! Sometimes I have to go back to where I was to trigger the thought I initially had.

The following chapters explore how to define happiness for yourself and some common pitfalls to avoid if you can (unless you absolutely insist on doing things the hard way)! We also need to clarify a few things about happiness, such as once you create your plan and carry it out arriving at long last in Happyland, does this give you a lifetime membership? Um, sorry. No lifetime memberships. But, I do have some good news!

You get a Visa!

You can visit Happyland as much as you want, it's just that sometimes life might ask you to leave for a bit to get your ass kicked before you can come back. But you do get to come back if you so choose! I know, that totally sucks but it's the nature of happiness and of life, really. Experiences help us grow and it is essential we do not become stagnant. The ups and downs allow us to appreciate the good because we have fought through the bad. There are opposing forces, mindsets and behaviors at work constantly as I have already explained. Furthermore, experience is what brings about change. Sometimes, you need the lesson and the experience in order to make the changes that will take you to new places. You can't change if you stop moving.

Chapter 4:
WHAT DOES HAPPINESS MEAN TO YOU?

What does happiness mean to you? And I really mean, JUST YOU. When you think about this, please try to not let the opinions of others influence your definition. You will likely have some sort of internal dialogue while you think this through. You will come up with a great part of your happiness definition and then you will hear "that voice" break into your head trying to convince you your definition sucks. Just tell it to shut up and leave the room so you can get back at it. If that voice keeps breaking in, it is a sure sign that you are living your life "under the influence," and you worry about what others will think about your choices. Happy people do not seek out the approval of others. They do not compare themselves to others. They do not surround themselves with a social network that is going to do its best to ruin them. Your choices are your choices. **How**

you define happiness determines how you will know when you achieve it. This is a critical step. Be bold.

This might be the hardest part: gaining clarity around what happiness means to YOU without being influenced by social conditioning or the expectations of others. You have to be a bit brave and somewhat bold to define this for yourself. You also have to be a wee bit fearless because what makes you happy might actually disappoint others. But, as we learn later, other people's happiness is NOT your responsibility. This means you also have to know a little bit about what is your responsibility and what is not. I will discuss that more in Part 3. For now, let's just start with defining happiness for you.

Sonja Lyubomirsky's research revealed that happiness is made of two components: meaning (purpose) and pleasure (positive emotions). In other words, you have created meaning or discovered your purpose in life and you are pulling pleasure from your journey as you move towards your goals. Tal Ben-Shahar states "Happiness isn't about reaching the peak of a mountain or climbing aimlessly around it. It is the experience of climbing towards that peak." It's a slight twist to see it that way but it does, indeed, make a difference. Many years ago, I thought happiness would arrive when I had checked things off my amazing life list: good job, life partner, kids... but I also used to think happiness was just a feeling. I strived to feel happy. Now, for me, I understand that feeling happiness is a by-product of how I think and act. It doesn't just happen; you have to create it for yourself.

Social psychologist Jonathan Haidt discusses a definition for happiness in his book *The Happiness Hypothesis* that I absolutely love. He explains that many people believe happiness comes from within. I do believe this from the standpoint that it is YOUR responsibility to create happiness, and that only you can determine what makes you happy, but he goes a little deeper. He also explains that a person who experiences the ups and downs does, in fact, eventually evolve to greater levels of happiness because the suffering, so to speak, allows them to experience happiness on a more profound level. Let's hold a little celebration here because now we can be sincerely thankful for all those shitty days and experiences! Experiencing both forces, such as triumph and failure makes us appreciate the highs more and it helps us understand lows are temporary. I can certainly vouch that this has been my own personal experience. I am a much stronger and happier person because of the "training" I have endured to get here. Do you find truth in this for your own life?

But wait, that's not all! Haidt makes magic happen when he further explains that happiness comes from the relationships **between** three things: yourself and others, yourself and your work, and yourself and something larger than yourself. I love this definition because it is so chewy and it accounts for so many variables. **Happiness comes from between.** Thank you Jonathan! Whether you agree with this or not, it does give you a few things to consider when creating your own definition of happiness. Like, for example, we do not exist in isolation from others and we are connected to so many things — we live in fact between many moving parts.

Given all these juicy morsels of insight into how we might define happiness, I would ask you to consider how you define happiness for yourself. Do you believe in order to be happy you need to have things? Do you believe you need goals? Do you believe you need purpose? Do you believe you need relationships and connections? Do you believe you need a partner?

What is your own personal definition of happiness?
Perhaps a good way to begin this activity is to brainstorm what you feel brings you happiness, or moments when you feel pleasure, purpose and meaning. There is no right answer to this, and I think the answer changes as we grow and experience things. Wisdom can change what brings you pleasure. I know that one of the happiest moments of my life was the birth of my daughter (I was not awake for the birth of my son just in case he reads this and claims I have favorites,) but there was no physical pleasure in her birth experience. In fact, it was incredibly scary and painful. However, I was twisted into that moment so tightly I couldn't separate myself from it in any way. When they placed this beautiful child into my arms, I almost couldn't process my emotions. I was totally blissed out (blessed + bliss.) In some of the early days with my son, having finally realized my dream of becoming a mother, I found myself incredibly content and at peace. He was such a calm and cuddly baby that I found nothing but joy holding and loving him, amazed he was finally here, and stunned that two regular people could create something so precious.

Likewise, when I ran my first marathon I was so fricking happy that I had managed to get to the point where I would even attempt a 26.2-mile run. The first three miles seemed so easy as I was carried along by the twenty thousand other runner's excitement. At eight miles, I was a little more realistic.

At twenty miles, I was not happy, far from it in fact. My friend Cookie kept telling me it was time to run again, and all I could think about was that if I didn't look down towards my feet, I wouldn't see my shin bones pushing through the tops of my knee caps. I was in agony! By mile twenty-two, I was talking to myself and having conversations with GOD. I encouraged Cookie to run ahead because at this point I hated her. I have told her that, too. We laugh now, but at that moment I was ass deep in misery and my nerves were raw! The man who ran with a jingle bell attached to his fanny pack was about to become a victim of homicide because I had listened to that damn bell dingle for over five hours. When I finally crossed that finish line I was blissed the fuck out. I have never been so relieved in all my life to be able to stop running. Truth be told, what I was doing was not really running, it was slogging, but who cares? I finished. I was elated.

While Karen and I had a post-race snack and discussed the possibility of safely removing our socks without the soles of our feet coming along with them, I may have even experienced euphoria. We wandered down to the ocean to put our feet in the water and when I did, seven out of ten toenails lifted off my nail bed each time a wave rolled in. I stood there stunned as my loose toenails flapped in the waves and the horror of what I had done to myself set in. Does any part of this scenario I have described really sound like I was happy? Yet, I was. I was proud. I was exhausted. I was content, relieved, and I was happy.

Defining happiness for yourself is a process. When I work with clients, we start with examining their values. While this seems relatively simple, it can be difficult for people to nail down what it is they want, what they desire, and what they feel passionate about. They are trying to figure it out using old constructs, social conditioning, and often the voice of someone else is in their head fighting them at every turn. We really need to lean on our creativity and intuition. We need to start asking ourselves questions that we do not normally ask ourselves if we want different answers. We need to create answers from scratch, and by that I mean from our own hearts. **To feel fully alive, you must walk through life awake. Likewise, to be happy you must define it for yourself and understand its nature so you can be aware of the happiness already within you.**

{If you find that you struggle here and you need some structure to walk you through the process, I have a short online video course that explains step-by-step where to begin and how to move forward on this. *The OMG Sessions* are in a self-paced, home study format so you can move along at your own pace. You can find more information at www.swiftkicklife.com}

Chapter 5:

THE EBB AND FLOW OF HAPPINESS

After a long, cold Canadian winter the first day of spring finally arrives and I find myself savoring the warmth of the sun. Happiness is a bit like that. There is an ebb and flow to your state of happiness so your gratitude for it remains. Part of the beauty in appreciating happiness is that if you have ever been without it, you cherish the happiness and contentment at an entirely new level. Your ability to experience happiness becomes more intense.

You understand while you may not be happy every minute of every day, for the majority of the time you are a happy person. You know when you feel sad that you will feel happy again. You understand that you need to move through things and experiences to move deeper into happiness.

In Psychology Today's *What Happy People Do Differently* researchers state that "we don't deny the importance of happiness—but we've also concluded a well-lived life is more than just one in which you feel 'up.' The good life is best construed as a matrix that includes happiness, occasional sadness, a sense of purpose, playfulness, and psychological flexibility, as well autonomy, mastery, and belonging."

Happiness is a matrix. How you arrange these connected elements (work, relationships, self-care, mindset, actions, and experiences) is entirely up to you. It doesn't mean that the ebb and flow stops. There is a natural rhythm to things, cycles to life, relationships, and anything you have a place in between. The sun comes up and it sets, the tide rolls in and recedes, and your happiness level will never hold still but you certainly can raise the bar. Elements in your matrix are moving and changing all the time, but a happiness mindset can hold them all together.

"The truth is that in order for you to experience true happiness in your life, you must experience sadness. It's required. Without sadness, we really can't even understand what happiness is." ~ Karl Moore

Chapter 6:
RESPONSIBILITY

Do you have a problem? I did.

❧❧

"If your happiness depends on what somebody else does, I guess you do have a problem." ~ Richard Bach

❧❧

I had *that* problem and it made for some pretty tricky living. I have said time and time again that accepting responsibility changes the game completely. (After all, the first step to solving a problem is acknowledging you have one.) But many stay locked in the routine of blame and, in doing so, remain captive to the victim mindset and lack of personal control. The flip side of this is many of us also believe we are responsible for the happiness of others. I have no idea how this happens but many people have the tendency to adopt responsibilities that do not belong to them. In terms of happiness alone, just think about what you do on a daily basis to make others happy. **It's fine to be giving and generous towards others and to do what you can to make others happy, but not at the risk of your own freedoms and happiness.** And, most certainly, not out of fear.

ॐॐ

"You must love in such a way that the person you love feels free." ~ Thích Nhất Hạnh

ॐॐ

Are you loved in such a way that you feel free to dream of things that make you happy and are able to work towards making these things a reality? Are you supported to create happiness in your life even if others have to step up to the plate and take responsibility for the creation of their own happiness?

ॐॐ

"A belief is not an idea held by the mind, it is an idea that holds the mind." ~ Elly Roselle

ॐॐ

If you believe you are responsible for the happiness of others or your happiness is dependent on other people, this belief will hold you prisoner, claim your control and keep you stuck. Joel

Osteen nails it: "You weren't created to be unhappy in order to keep everyone else happy."

I was chatting with a woman who was stuck in a miserable marriage. She was bitter and adamantly declared that she was taught to believe this was how it should be (social conditioning). She also told me she would be teaching her children differently. Yet, she stayed. She modeled exactly the behavior she wanted to teach her children to avoid. She was miserable. I am sure her husband was as well because she was filled with so much hate and anger. But what she didn't seem to recognize was that it was absolutely in her power to change things, to adjust her sail and to model for her children that happiness was her personal responsibility. I understand that fear, guilt, conditioning, and finances may have also been at work here but ultimately staying would never bring her happiness.

If you have children, what behaviors do you exhibit that may be teaching them (via modeling) something exactly opposite of what you wish for them to learn? What about the lessons you learned observing others?

You must establish personal control over your own life. Other people should not be allowed the power to dictate the way you live your life. Instead, strive to establish personal control in your life, which in turn will allow you to fulfill your own goals and dreams. Personal control will also increase your sense of personal self-worth.

Chapter 7:

WHAT COMES FIRST?

Where does happiness start? Do you become happy when you have acquired everything that you think will make you happy? Or, do you learn to become happy and then success follows?

There is endless discussion in positive psychology circles about what brings about happiness. Recent research by Shawn Achor and many others suggests success does not actually bring about happiness. In fact, Achor argues that happiness fuels success, not the other way around. When we are positive, our brains become more engaged, creative, motivated, energetic, resilient and productive.

Therefore, focusing on creating happiness in your life now, where you are, with what you have, is essential. By learning to be happy on purpose, you become more engaged and resilient which in turn makes you happier. This triggers things to happen that bring you success. It isn't the success that brings you happiness unless you are happy first.

Chapter 8:
NO PERMISSION REQUIRED

"You are not the boss of me!" I have heard this screamed across school playgrounds for fifteen years. Five year olds get it on some level, that they have a right to free will and no one else can be the "boss of them."

Some adults struggle with this for decades. Social conditioning works its magic on our thinking patterns and convinces us we should seek out the approval of others before we act. The biggest favor I ever did myself was simply to let that go. I realized I didn't need anyone else's approval about how I decided to create a life for myself. If the consequences for my choices were to be mine alone, so then should the choices about what I decided to do and how I decided to think.

❧❧

"Most of us believe in trying to make other people happy only if they can be happy in ways in which we approve." ~ Robert Staughton Lynd

❧❧

It's important to follow your own dreams and desires without letting naysayers stand in your way. It's fine to seek others' opinions, but happy people stay true to their own hearts and don't get bogged down with the need for outside approval. A quote I absolutely love that ties several of the previous points together into an intricate summary is this one below.

❧❧

"Everything changes when you start to emit your own frequency rather than absorbing the frequencies around you, when you start imprinting your intent on the universe rather than receiving an imprint from existence." ~ Barbara Marciniak.

❧❧

Setting a daily intention is a practice that is woven into my Signature LIFEMAP Program because it is such a powerful behavior. Setting intentions really does help you deflect the persuasion of others. It also protects you against the intrusion of your environment to manipulate you to feel, act and think in another way. It takes some practice but when you learn to set intentions, you are far more likely to stay focused on your own journey and goals and way less likely to seek out the permission of others and stray from your own purpose.

Chapter 9:
A WAY OF TRAVEL

We always hear the phrase, "life is about the journey and not the destination." Quite frankly, if you think about that one long and hard enough it makes complete sense. The journey *is* the process of living and the destination very well could be death. Therefore, happiness and the way you choose to see the world really becomes your way of travel to the ultimate place of rest. I don't know about you, but I insist on having a fabulous time getting to the end! Roll out the red carpet because I am going to dance my ass from one end to the other. Join me!

True happiness can be found in the way you approach life. It is the perspective you have consistently on the external events in your world, and you are in control of this. Perspective is your choice. While it might be true your life sucks, that doesn't mean you need to rot in unhappiness. You may be poor, but there are poor happy people all over the world. You just might be over-looking the riches you currently do have. **You might be trying**

to collect happiness in the wrong currency. Is happiness a fat wallet or loving and supportive family and friends? It doesn't matter to me what your answer is, just that you are living in line with your values. If your currency is a supportive and loving social network but you spend your time chasing the almighty dollar, will you ever find happiness even if you succeed in bagging millions? No, it is like collecting apples when you need oranges.

You can consciously create happiness by understanding YOUR happiness currency because while society might say the happiness currency is the good job, nice house and cool car, I challenge you to determine if you are functioning under the same definition. If you are, great! You can function in society and follow "their rules" and create happiness for yourself. But if you operate on a different currency then you will need to be brave, bold and creative to figure out how you will navigate your way through this life on your terms, using your own happiness currency.

Your life might suck, but that doesn't mean you can't be happy. Happiness is the way you perceive the world. If happiness is a currency, are you collecting the right kind?

Chapter 10:
WE HAVE A SITUATION

When I was visiting Jamaica a few years ago, I was enthralled with the playful banter of a local citizen. One thing he said that made me laugh but stuck in my head like a bad rap song was, "In Jamaica, we do not have problems, we have situations!"

Whaaaat?

I knew the minute I heard that phrase my take on problems had forever been shifted. Again, this is all about perspective. You know when the shit hits the fan and you suddenly realize you "have a problem" to deal with? You can hear that voice inside your head yapping almost immediately. "Oh, we have a huge problem!" I hear my kids say it, "Mom, I have a problem!" My students say it, "I have this little problem."

You might even pick up the phone and tell someone else about your problem, embellishing your description of all the additional

48

issues and hardships that will come your way as a result of this horrible problem. To add a little more zing you might use really emotional words to describe what's going on further feeding the problem and everyone's emotional reaction to the event.

Wait! It isn't a problem. It is an opportunity to stretch yourself and test your creativity. It's merely a change in the situation. Calling it a problem brings with it negative connotations. Baggage. Judgment.

What you have here is merely a situation, an opportunity, and possibly a change in direction. When you start viewing problems differently, they become less earth- shattering and more a part of life. Problems can be opportunities. They don't have to derail you.

PART 3:
The Practice of Happiness

Achieving happiness is much like looking through a kaleidoscope. The picture (and your happiness level) can change quickly with a few movements on the kaleidoscope barrel. Knowing that, pace yourself. Pick a couple of the strategies I suggest below that resonate with you. Do not strive for perfection, strive to pay attention to what works for you and what does not. Create your custom design.

This is where the rubber hits the road so to speak. Time and time again you will hear me say there is a difference between knowing what needs to be done and actually DOING it. Lots of people know what they need to do to lose weight. They don't do it. They don't change their behavior. They don't commit to DOING what it takes to make the change. Others might know that a relationship needs to change but they don't act on that knowledge because something holds them back (fear, anxiety or judgment of others).

The more research I did into the science of happiness, the more I found that happy people do things differently. There are numerous little tools and tricks but I decided to start with the things that worked for me. Not only does this allow me to provide you with concrete examples why I decided to do something, but I can also explain how I did things. You get the *all-access pass* into the thought processes that evolved as I moved through various approaches. I think it is worthwhile to have that all-access pass because life doesn't happen in a laboratory and we all have spouses, children, jobs, messy houses, obligations, and other distractions that can play into how well we can implement some of these strategies.

The following strategies are the things I consciously DID to change my mindset, my behaviors, and as a result, my life. I DID THEM. They worked only when I decided to DO the work. They can work for you too IF you implement them. I consider it a super big perk that the field of positive psychology and research on happiness supports what I did on my own. It actually makes me feel pretty darn smart until I remind myself it took me a decade to figure it out. We are trying to skip the suffering part of all this for you!

I mentioned earlier, achieving happiness is much like looking through a kaleidoscope. The picture (and your happiness level) can change quickly with a few movements on the kaleidoscope barrel. Knowing that, pace yourself. Pick a couple of strategies I suggest below that resonate with you and start. Do not strive for perfection, strive to pay attention to what works for you and what does not. Create your beautiful, personal, smile-inducing design.

Remember, in an effort to support you and to provide some additional actionable items that are ready for you to use, I created a companion resource to this book called *The HAPPYPACK*. You can download this resource for free from my website, www. swiftkicklife.com. The details for downloading *The HAPPYPACK* are in the section about the Companion Resource.

Okay, let's kick this all into gear shall we?

Chapter 11:
GRATITUDE

Gratitude has saved my sanity. Gratitude has extended some serious support when the stress in my life was at an all-time high. Gratitude has given me hope and lightened my load even when I felt hopeless and overwhelmed. Gratitude has taught me about faith.

I wish I had been aware of the practice of gratitude when I found myself going through my divorce. I know, without a doubt, it would have helped me move through it faster. I mean, I was aware of gratitude because Oprah always talked about it, but I do recall rolling my eyes at the idea. It wasn't until I was truly desperate that I opened myself up to the possibility it could help me. It seemed so simple, I just didn't understand how it could make a difference. Well, breathing is simple too, right? And it makes a HUGE difference to my well-being!

It is the very first thing I tell everyone who asks "What can I do right now to increase my sense of happiness?" The impact of practicing gratitude can be absolutely profound and rather immediate. Remember, to feel a certain way we need to consider the mindset AND the actions we take to create the resulting feeling. Being grateful for even the simplest things encourages us to act differently and that change in behavior brings about an increased sense of well-being without anything else having changed.

I won't go into details (the long version of the story is in my other book) but I first started using gratitude to gain some control and perspective over my life when my daughter started having seizures and my life started to spiral out of control. My nerves were shot. I had so much anxiety about her health that I could barely function. Not to mention I was sleep-deprived beyond measure because these seizures required constant supervision. There was only one of me and let's just say I was in deep. Here is an example how practicing gratitude can take a stressful situation and shift your focus to something good and beautiful.

It was a long day. A long, hard day. Bean had a seizure at school today in the hallway. A sad milestone for her because it was a big one, and the first seizure she couldn't hide from her peers with EMS arriving to assist. I can't imagine how it feels to be slowly clawing your way to consciousness in a fluctuating state of confusion and fear while strange faces peered at you with genuine concern. I could see so many emotions flash across her sweet, beautiful face in those fleeting moments that others wouldn't have noticed. I wanted to hold her but I knew she wasn't ready. She cried in the car and didn't want me to take her to the hospital to have her checked out. And, with each of her exasperated, frustrated, angry cries my heart broke and my will to fix everything recoiled into the corner to allow her the space to work through what had happened today. When we arrived home, she went into the house without speaking.

She is sleeping now, curled up holding her head, in an attempt to make it hurt less. I am listening to the deep, soft breaths she is taking and finding comfort that she is now home with me, and that we are tucked safely into our comfortable little sanctuary together, able to settle into the post-seizure routine we have come to know as normal. I never thought I could love like this.

As the light from the hallway pushes into the room and dances across her face, I see nothing but my baby resting there. Her long beautiful eyelashes and whipped butter skin. Her hair has gently settled across her cheeks. She might be fifteen years old, but her hands still look like toddler hands when held at her temples in sleep. I reach out and stroke her warm skin and am amazed again how this beautiful child has taught me to love so incredibly deeply. I am so blessed to have her in my life and to be the one who cares for her when she is in need. I leave her room and pull the door shut, and my heart overflows with joy that she belongs to me. I am so lucky to be blessed with this child, her beauty, her intelligence, and her amazing spirit. Today was not a great day, but she is safely resting now. Tomorrow is a new day. Regardless of today's events, I am blessed and I am happy.

Gratitude has this amazingly powerful way of teaching your brain how to sort the external world and focus on what brings you happiness, joy, pleasure and peace. When totally overwhelmed, our brains have to decide what we let into our consciousness. Gratitude helps us create a filter. While I could have slipped into panic mode and focused on the seizure, instead I concentrated on how grateful I was for her in my life. If you focus on good, you see more good. Good things soon appear to be everywhere even though the stressful stuff hasn't vanished. **You learn to lean into the good.** It holds you up. Gratitude helps you control your focus on what is going on around you. Think of the practice of gratitude like a bag: there is only so much room in the bag and gratitude helps you decide what to put in the bag. As we discussed earlier, to avoid fear you can choose gratitude. Actively doing so changes your outlook very quickly.

Gratitude also puts a pretty quick stop to the practice of feeling sorry for oneself. Without gratitude you can be overly focused on the shit and you don't see any of the sunshine. A daily practice of gratitude is also part of my Signature LIFEMAP Program because it is such a simple, yet powerful tool. It helps us live in the moment and wakes us to the blessing in our lives. It also helps us understand that situations are always temporary and dynamically moving around us, a part of a much larger picture.

I speak so much about gratitude that people must wonder why I keep harping on the issue. Quite simply, when I first heard about the practice of gratitude I laughed it off because I didn't really understand the entire concept. I don't want you to do the same. When I finally started integrating gratitude into my life, things changed rapidly. And, I might add my life still sucked but my happiness began to increase and my stress level and anxiety became manageable despite the circumstance I was living in at the time.

❦ ❧

"Blessed are they who see beautiful things in humble places where other people see nothing." ~ Camille Pissarro

❦ ❧

Now it is your turn. Grab your free *HAPPYPACK* from www.swiftkicklife.com and get started! (I have included a 21-Day Gratitude Journal as part of this resource.)

Chapter 12:
LET GO

There is a definite difference between telling yourself you are going to let go of things (only to make snide remarks or behave passive aggressively by slamming down dishes and coffee cups) and actually letting go. The former might have you going through the motions, you may even begin to hide your emotions in an effort to appear successful, but the latter allows you to let go from the heart. Letting go at the heart level means you accept what has taken place, cherish the lessons, acknowledge the good and the bad, and then move forward without anything holding you back.

Back in the day I was really good at pretend-letting go. I clung to things like I was drowning in an angry ocean. These past events had somehow become my story and my lifeline, but little did I realize they were in fact, my anchor. I collected anchors! My boat was full! No wonder life was hard!

I think that many people struggle with letting go because broken hearts and disappointment are almost always involved. I thought I had let go of many things in my life but to truly understand how this lightens the load, you have to experience it just once. I wasn't aware that I was pretend-letting go, until I was successful at my first true release. **This first experience came when I realized that in order to let go and forgive, I had to release the judgments I held in my own mind about the people who I felt hurt me and their actions that I deemed hurtful.** I realized that every time I thought about this event, I replayed my judgment and it was no longer the event but my judgment that held me captive.

Once I had experienced successfully letting go of something, I realized how partial my previous efforts had been. I sensed a very different relief when I let go for real.

Previously, I had struggled with thinking if I let go of things completely it somehow meant I had been lying about the significance in the first place. I also thought some people didn't deserve my forgiveness. But then I learned forgiveness was a gift I could give myself. Forgiveness means you don't have room in your heart for the things that bring you down. As I mentioned before, Buddha's wise words capture the importance of letting go *for real*, "Holding onto anger is like drinking poison and expecting the other person to die."

Let go. Free yourself. Lighten your load. Stop judging. Before you let go, grab the lessons of significance and then let your anchor sink without you attached to it.

Chapter 13:
LIVE WITH LESS

I was visiting with a healer one day and conversation mean-dered to the topic of happiness. I began explaining how my divorce and the subsequent distribution of assets had taught me a few important lessons about "stuff" and "things." The initial years of my marriage found me spending my time and energy working towards the accumulation and acquisition of things: degrees, a home, items for the home, a car, and then a more desirable car and so on. It never stopped, as there was always something else to work towards. Then, along came the separation and a divorce. We all know how that story goes.

Once items had been removed from the walls and rooms par-tially emptied of stuff, I panicked in the empty space. I wasn't comfortable with it at all. Bare walls. Simplicity. Memories bounced around off the walls like loose balls in a pinball machine. It seemed so void of life and warmth. I had to really fight the desire to just fill the room back up with more mean-ingless stuff. I wanted to stifle the echo of my pain so badly.

Instead, I left it and grew to become comfortable with the sim-plicity. (To be honest, I was just too damn tired to deal with it.) I tossed around ideas about what type of home environment I wanted to create and took my time crafting the feel. I played lots of music. I wandered through the now empty spaces and worked hard to assign a new vibe to them.

I painted walls. I opted for burnt orange, deep reds, and earth tones. The colour was refreshing and soothing all at the same time. It changed the mood of my home. I moved on to furni-ture. I kept what I loved and moved items to new places. I split up the bedroom furniture and the pieces became new again in fresh rooms. I focused on creating places to gather and talk with my kids and friends. I added new art and quotes to the walls. I surrounded myself with inspiration and reminders of the new life I was creating for myself. It was certainly a process and it continues to be one. Slowing down and taking my time with the space and the stuff taught me several things.

1. **Items in my environment can trigger emotional responses in me.** I wasn't always aware of what exactly was happening but I knew I felt off, where moments before I had been fine. Stuff can hold memories. Stuff can hold onto bad energy. If you keep walking past an item that used to signify something important to you and now it reminds you of something that makes you sad, you have an energy problem.

2. **The more stuff I had, the more stress I seemed to have.** I had stuff all over that wasn't really important to me, but it seemed wasteful to throw it away. I struggled with wasting money and resources when my future seemed uncertain and had a hard time giving things up.

3. **When I realized my extra stuff could be someone else's fresh start, I began giving stuff away.** Following my initial kick-ass house purge, I felt so much lighter and carefree. The healer summed it up like this, "For every little thing you own, it owns a piece of you!" I LOVED THAT! Thank you Brenda Hanson!

If you have a bunch of "stuff" it does take time and energy to manage it. If you have a few boxes of stuff in your closet you need to move every time you want a clean towel, that stuff robs you of a few seconds and a bit of energy each time you have to move them. If you add up the efforts it takes to contend with all your stuff on a day-to-day basis, you begin to see why stuff can truly own a piece of you. If you have clutter in a closet that falls out and jams the door every time you open it to look for something, you have a pain in the ass and an energy drain. If you have a bunch of clothes that you don't wear, you create an environment where the clothes you DO love get lost. You have to then spend the time sorting through the closets looking for the clothes you feel best in. Why do that? Why not ... wait for it ... just have clothes you love. It seems so simple.

Less is so triumphantly more.

Chapter 14:
R & R

I know you are thinking rest and relaxation when you see R & R but what I mean is Record and Reflect. When I was a teenager, and nothing but an acne covered mood swing, I spent many hours writing poetry and journaling. I recorded good things that were part of my journey through those teen years and I worked through negative things that happened as well. I also made it a ritual to go back and read previous entries at a later date to see how my thoughts and feelings had changed.

It always surprised me to read my journal. Did I really write that? It was always like I was reading someone else's words and the more time that had passed since the entry, the more removed I often felt from it and the more clarity I found. I was evolving as a human even as I wrote and worked through things. Having this record of my journey and my thoughts made me considerably more reflective of what created lasting change, happiness, or sadness in my life. I learned to recognize patterns and became much more aware of myself.

When I was seventeen and fresh out of high school, I moved to the mountains and became a chambermaid at a high-end resort. Shortly after arriving, I moved up to breakfast waitress and spent several months clearing tables, pouring coffee and sneaking bacon off the buffet. When that lifestyle began to lose its appeal, I planned an epic adventure for myself, oblivious to possible dangers of traveling alone as a young girl. At least in my planning, I picked a country where they spoke English so that I wouldn't have any language barriers! But if you have ever heard a string of accented slag roll off the tongue of an Aussie, you know I walked blindly into a whole new world!

I travelled solo to Australia on a student visa when I was barely eighteen. With my backpack and some cash, I landed in Australia and then realized I didn't have any idea what I was supposed to do. While opportunities for adventures surrounded me, the first few months I spent keeping cautiously to myself. I found a job, made some friends, stopped crying myself to sleep at night and ended up understanding it was entirely up to me to create a year to remember. I started journaling and recording my days because new things happened so quickly and I didn't want to forget anything. I also wrote letters home to my parents. This was before email and Skype. (That makes me sound so old!)

Mom kept all the letters and when I found the box of letters and my journals a few years back, I sat quietly for hours and relived every moment of my time traveling abroad that year. I had a smile from ear to ear re-living what had turned out to be one of the most important years of my young life. I could see through my own words, how I had grown, changed and matured while I was away. I couldn't believe some of the stuff I did. I remember my father saying I wouldn't come back the same person and he was so right.

As I moved through my life, I would return to journaling when I began to feel myself losing my way. Little did I know it at the time, but my pen and paper had become a powerful life tool. Writing allowed me to clarify my thoughts and feelings, identify and then maneuver past mental blocks. It helped me understand myself better. It helped my see the things I was "between" and my role in their dysfunction or their bliss.

When I was writing in my Australian journal, I remember specifically re-reading an entry about an event that had taken place between me and my boyfriend at the time. Several months had passed since the initial entry and I had gone back to re-read it. The journal entry became a catalyst for an amazing Australian adventure. As I moved through my own thoughts and descriptions of what had taken place, my heart grew heavy as I suddenly realized my boyfriend was a total asshole. Re-reading the entry had backed me out of the relationship enough for me to see things differently than I had when I was IN the event I had written about. My friends had told me I deserved better, and finally I saw exactly what they meant. **I never lied to the paper and in turn, it took care of me.**

I instantly called up my friend who had been suggesting we quit our jobs and tour up the coast of Australia together for a few months before I flew home. I told her I was game. I packed my bags, she bought a tent, and we both gave notice. The only thing I regret was that I hadn't read that journal entry a month or two sooner because I had felt like I had wasted valuable time during my year abroad!

Within a week, I hopped on the back of my friend's motorcycle and off we went with all our stuff tethered to the back rack. In the months that followed we explored the Australian coast, made new friends, found trouble, and wiggled our way out of it time and time again. When the floodwaters made the motorcycle an impossible mode of transport, we parked it and used our thumbs. We slept on the back of semi-trailers loaded with tarped potatoes, ate meals in truck stops with our new friends, and chartered a small plane to take us to Fraser Island for a weekend camping adventure -- citing the fact that we would never have the chance to do this again and we were both too young to rent a 4x4 (thank goodness for credit cards).

As we hiked from the airstrip to the campsite, we nearly crapped our pants when we could hear something very large smashing quickly in the brush. It was a reptile of some kind, but to this naïve prairie girl it had to be a croc so I kept damn close to the centerline of the trail so I could move quickly in either direction if I needed to flee. We watched a herd of wild brumbies gallop majestically across and open field (they have since been removed from the island and I am forever grateful for that experience) and I accidentally let a couple timid dingoes into our tent when I had left it to throw up in the bush from over consumption of boxed wine and under consumption of food and fresh water. At first, I thought it was incredibly funny until we noticed one of us was missing a shoe. (Ok, it wasn't my shoe so it was actually really funny.) Thankfully, a young couple took pity on us and drove us to the airstrip to meet the plane for departure. My friend might have drowned me if she had to hike through the bush with only one shoe!

That trip was about twenty-five years ago but journaling about it has presented me with the memories and the lessons that I can replay over and over again. (I don't drink boxed wine in large quantities anymore.) Looking back over these journals taught me I was a brave young girl with an incredible zest for life. **Imagine the gift these journals gave me when I sat down to read them as a broken, sad, wife and mother who doubted her strength and ability.** I somehow had become the main character in my own adventure story and I became reacquainted with the fiery young girl who I had lost along the way. My journals gave me hope for something better in the darkest days of my adult life.

Take the time to record and reflect.

Chapter 15:
BE KIND

Shawn Achor claims that altruism helps fights depression. I tried a little experiment of my own and although the jury is still out on how this experiment ends, it was a shitload of fun.

❧ ❧

"Thousands of candles can be lit from a single candle, and the life of the candle will not be shortened. Happiness is never decreased by being shared." ~Buddha

❧ ❧

When I began writing this book, I had an idea for testing this strategy out. We have all heard of random acts of kindness and the pay-it-forward movement based in the idea that if one person does something kind for someone else; a ripple effect of kindness begins. So, I printed 100 Kindness Cards. On the cards I asked people to visit the 100kindnesscards.com website I created to record their card number and the circumstances around how they received the card and how they intended to pay it forward.

I have handed out about half of the cards, and the website has some seriously heartwarming stories on it to read about the acts of kindness that were part of my ripple. But many people have not reported their cards or events with the website yet because they didn't understand what the card asked of them, they were part of the generation who has no idea what www means, they forgot, they haven't paid it forward yet or they simply didn't bother. It doesn't really matter because my daughter and I had lots of fun watching people receive our random acts of kindness, most of which we were able to pull off anonymously!

Perhaps the most moving story recorded to date on the www.100kindnesscard.com website was one from lady named Roberta.

"Thank you for doing this. I was having the worst day ever, lost in my own funk of complaining and I was walking around like a dark cloud. And then, I lost my bankcard in the machine. I was running late. This lovely lady stopped what she was doing to try to help me get my card back. I was on the verge of tears. She looked at me and told me that it looked like I was having a shit day and said when she has these days she stops and takes a couple deep breaths. She told me her kids thought she was a wacko but now they tell her to breathe. So she started breathing and I followed.

We laughed.

It broke the bubble of badness. She handed me a card and told me to make the most of the day I had left, little things don't matter, and she adjusted her oxygen tank and walked away. This has changed my life." (From 100kindnescards.com)

When I read this, I smiled. The hair on my arms stood up and I had a glimpse at how powerful a movement like this can be. I didn't know this woman. Somehow one of my cards made it to her through another woman and changed her life! That is huge. That feels amazing!

If you would like to give this a little whirl, invent your own movement or create your own cards and send them to the 100kindnesscards.com. I will approve any appropriate (and clean) messages that spread kindness. There are endless ways to start your own ripple: Smile at someone. Say good morning to someone you meet on the sidewalk and make eye contact. What happens to you when you see your smile makes a difference to someone else? Neuroscience research on the Greater Good website shows when people practice kindness, our brains actually light up in areas associated with pleasure and reward. It is a reward for us to practice kindness so don't hold back, reward yourself!

Be sincere. Buy someone a coffee. Pay the bill of the person behind you in the drive-thru. Open a door or help someone with a heavy load. Offer someone a ride. Take coffee or treats to an office you frequent. Write someone a heartfelt note. Sit with a single senior and give him or her the gift of your time and attention, you will walk away better for it. Don't believe me? Read on!

One day I was quickly checking Facebook and I stumbled across Cara's post. It was one of the longest posts I had ever seen but I stopped to read it. I loved the message so much that I asked Cara if I could include it in my book. It just made me stop and think. Her message reminded me of my own local Starbucks and an elderly gentleman I would see there from time to time. He would sit alone and have his special drink. Sometimes he would bring a book and other times he wouldn't. When he didn't have his book, I always wondered if he was looking for a human connection instead. One day I arrived at Starbucks to do some work and couldn't find an empty table. I decided to ask if I could join him and he lit up to have the company. I knew there would be no work done that day. Anyway, I digress. Here is Cara's story.

> *I'm not sure where to begin here-- Just another day in the life of your average freelance graphic designer. However, today I wanted out of my window-less office, (it's entirely too sunny and pleasant to be stuck in a dungeon) and I wasn't about to work from the kitchen where I, more than likely, would be capitulated to the chocolate chip cookies and snuggles of a small Yorkie. Not that I don't enjoy the localized hipster coffee joints, I just didn't want to deal with any of that today (you know what I mean) so I headed up to the rich-folk neighborhood Starbucks. My attitude was on high and I knew that I could get some work done to the tune of familiar triple shot lattes and a bit of Tone Loc that seemed to seep out of my coffee neighbors pocket as his iPhone rang.*

I set up shop. Tipped open my laptop, laid out my orange rugged LaCie external hard drive, connected my wireless mouse and opened up my design software.

"What kind laugh is that? Don't mothers teach their daughters to be lady-like anymore?" said the old man sitting near me. (Opposite the side of the "Wild Thang".) I turned to him knowing exactly what he was talking about. There were a few teenagers laughing like complete idiots a few feet away.

"I was honestly thinking that she sounded like a hyena as well," I said.

"I guess she's pretty happy, though. I'm reading a book on happiness, you know?" Said the well-dressed senior. "Can I read this part to you? I've underlined it."

I never turn anyone down who wants to converse with me. EVER. In fact, I encourage it because I love people of all sorts. I love their stories and have a bona fide interest in where they come from. (My specialty is strangers in airport bars.) Especially if it's a senior citizen, dressed to the nines, impeccable hair, that had an uncanny resemblance to Bob Barker.

"Of course you can!"

He reads me a few sentences from his Christian-esque book that indicated the happiness of humans.

I didn't really know where to go with this so I asked him about himself. He told me his name was Bob and for a few minutes, I really thought he was THE Bob Barker, you guys. Then, he goes on to tell me he's from Southern California, lived in Bel Air and Santa Barbara for a while. Sailed for fun, even had a 40' sailboat that he took seriously for about 10 years and was also a gymnast in his day. I honestly thought, "Maybe he IS BOB BARKER!"

Back and forth conversation, he also told me he was a Navy "Leap Frog" during the war. He was a handsome, elderly man that clearly took care of himself but I couldn't help but wonder if the scars on his face came from wartime. I asked the obvious questions and when someone tells me they are not a native Oklahoman, I itch to find out why they are here because I'm not native either. My mind immediately wanders to two reasons why they are here: the oil and gas industry or the Air Force. Aside from that, you're usually a native Oklahoman and love it here and never want to leave, or you're here because of a girl (or a guy).

Stricken with the wonder bug, I asked questions. It seemed he really wanted to talk. He said he's had a wonderful life, ultra-successful, made millions within the freight industry but got a divorce a while back while in California and his children, in the airline industry who live in Houston, put him in a retirement home out there.

He then told me was here because of a girl. I love how he said, "girl." He's probably pushing 90 years old, to me that was the cutest thing since baby Yorkies. He said she was wonderful.

"A pretty, little thing, too! I took her to dinner every night. She was so sweet. Buried 3 husbands, you know?" I could tell his tone grew heavy when he talked about her. His eyes welled up and I faced the past-tense of his speech. "She passed away of intestinal cancer and I just haven't left here because I recently had a stroke. I've lived in some beautiful places. I've gotten to experience beautiful things, but now I'm too old to go back so I enjoy riding my bike and studying up on the latest health trends and theology. I love theology," he said.

Bob went on to talk more about how he isn't facing old age that well. He said that his body doesn't want to cooperate with his mind much anymore. He said it's so frustrating to think that he was the "fittest of fit in the Navy," an incredible gymnast, sailed around the coast for 10 years, and the fact that he feels like he may fall down doesn't normally stop him, but it seems to scare him because it's harsh reality.

He looked at me and shook my hand. He said, "Go out and do it. Right now. Enjoy you. Enjoy what you love. Enjoy now. Remember the good things."

I can't wait to share with Jonathan.
(Story shared with permission by Cara Loper, Looselid Creative)

Now, I ask you to consider if Cara's extension of kindness lifted her up or brought her down. And Bob, how do you think he felt to have the companionship and connection with Cara that day?

Create your own ripple.

Chapter 16:
MOVE IT

Move any way you enjoy moving. Exercise is such a powerful tool for delivering an instant lift. Not only can exercise help you look better, it can do some pretty amazing things to your mental state. It can reduce the effects of stress, assist in fighting depression, improve learning and retention, build confidence and self-esteem, improve body image, and contribute to brain health. I know when I struggled exercise became my drug of choice, my coping mechanism, and my stress buster. I could definitely tell when it was time for a run. My children could too and if things grew too heavy in our home they would tell me to go run, or pass me my shoes. As author and Harvard Medical School psychiatrist John Ratey states in his book *Spark: The Revolutionary New Science of Exercise and the Brain*, "Exercise is the single best thing you can do for your brain in terms of mood, memory, and learning. Even ten minutes of activity changes your brain."

Wow! Not an hour – ten little minutes!

As a certified personal trainer, I give out advice all the time about how people can integrate movement into their daily lives. It doesn't need to be a run or a regular training plan, it just needs to be a consistent habit that you enjoy. If you have a dog, take your buddy for a stroll. If you have small kids, start walking instead of driving them to school. If you have a group of friends you never see, start a Talk & Walk club. If you have colleagues at work that want to get moving, do stair sets at breaks. Really the options are limited by your own imagination.

If you want to increase your strength, lift weights or do body weight exercises. If you can't get to a gym, create a space at home where you can do push-ups, lunges, and floor work of all kinds. Do it with your kids! Babies make great weights and it is fun for them too!

If you need some help getting started, check out the programs on my website. There are resources for the beginner (who doesn't know where to start or what to eat) right to the advanced athlete (who wants to push him or herself to new levels of fitness). Don't kill yourself; just make small changes overtime and in a few months your new habits will be fueling your mindset, changing your waistline, and your life!

Chapter 17:
FACE FEAR, SAY YES, TAKE ACTION

Fear gets a bad rap. Well, sometimes it does. It actually CAN be healthy and it can keep you out of harm's way. Your body is wired to pick up on things at a subconscious level like those chills that run up your spine when you talk to someone who might seem off but you can't explain why. There are a few times I can remember when my fear response fired up pretty quickly when things didn't feel quite right. While I couldn't explain what was off, my *fear-dar* knew something was wrong and fired up my flight or fight system with one swift shot of adrenaline. Mom, you should stop reading now.

{Thanks, Mom! Actually, it would be great if you just skipped ahead to the next chapter and hey, maybe take the kids with you?}

While on the same Australian adventure I talked about earlier, my girlfriend and I found ourselves just outside of the city on some rural roads trying to hitch a lift into town. (I know, bad idea.) A car load of guys drove past us yelling crude things out of the window. I hated it. I was scared. Sure, I took some risks but I usually thought them through and considered the possible outcomes. At heart, I was a big chicken but I also felt like I was in a bit over my head in this big old world. I told my friend we could just walk the few miles back into town. We were arguing about what to do when a car pulled up slowly, and the passenger asked us very politely if we needed a lift. She said yes and we both got in.

With four people already in the car, she took the front seat and I took the back seat on the opposite side of the car. Things were fine. There was polite conversation and small talk as we indicated where we wished to be dropped off. We drove in awkward silence for a while and then, the guy who was sitting in the back seat on the opposite side of the car started to laugh. My girlfriend looked back towards me. We both immediately seemed to be on high alert. My heart started to pulse against my chest. At the exact same moment we both realized what had happened and why riding in this car was suddenly a very bad idea.

The car full of heckling guys must have driven up the highway and taken an alternate road back to where they found us still walking. We had climbed into the car when they appeared well behaved, and now we were rolling down the highway trapped inside the car.

I was freaking terrified.
I immediately started looking for a way out. I slowly moved my hand to the door handle while my friend and I both continued to play dumb. The guy kept laughing and then the driver joined in. There was a weird vibe in the car.

My friend looked back towards me and signaled silently to look ahead. When I did I saw that we were approaching a stop sign close to the spot we had indicated we wanted to be dropped off. With her eyes, and a slight gesture with her head, she made it pretty damn clear we should jump from the car when it began to slow down.

I am not sure how this might have played out if we had not jumped from the car as it approached the stop sign. There were four large, young men in that car, none of which had any respect for women. When we both opened the doors and hit the pavement and they realized what we had done, they screamed out the windows at us and called us a plethora of nasty names. My friend grabbed my hand and we took off running towards the closest convenience store. Thinking of that incident 25 years later still causes my body to react with a sense of fear. And gratitude. I am quite certain I cannot capture in words exactly how dangerous the vibe felt. Words can't explain what my fear seemed to grasp that day.

However, I can also experience fear when it is just downright silly. For example, I am scared that fresh water fish might attack me if I swim in a lake. Legit. Being in a lake with that fear raging untamed can almost evoke the same reaction as the "hitchhiking gone bad" experience. The hitchhiking posed a real threat to my physical safety and my issue with fish is, well, somewhat based on my overactive imagination and exposure to the movie JAWS. However, this irrational fear of fish actually interferes with me doing what I want to do, therefore, it IS a block for me! It frustrates me and keeps me from living fully and taking part in things I want to do.

I am also scared of jumping from a perfectly good airplane with a parachute attached to my back. However, it is not on my bucket list and not a skill I require to live out my dreams so it is of no consequence to me. Being unable to skydive doesn't keep me from living to my full potential. This is something I can live with.

We must take a close look at the fears we have and decide which ones we need to try busting through. It has been said that all you need to make your dreams come true is waiting for you on the other side of fear. I believe it because when you take action and move through fear, you gain confidence. However, you need to focus on addressing the fears that actually inter-fere with living a full life, and not the ones designed to keep you safe or alert. Facing your fears, saying yes to life, and taking action facilitates progression forward. Moving through what keeps you stuck opens the world of possibilities. Do not let fear hold you back. Face the fear, uncertainty, and anxiety and act anyway. Say yes and then ACT on yes!

ϡϡ

"Death is not the biggest fear we have; our biggest fear is taking the risk to be alive—the risk to be alive and express what we really are." ~ Don Miguel Ruiz

ϡϡ

Do you fear fully living? I know at one time I sure did.

Chapter 18:
KEEP IT SIMPLE

Each year I pick a theme word for the year rather than a resolution. This works well for me because a theme allows me to integrate the goal into all areas of my life rather than just one area. For example, rather than lose weight, I choose healthy choices as a theme. I used to have resolutions and every year I failed to keep them. If I decide the theme is bliss then whenever I am faced with a choice, I just remind myself of the theme and it makes the choice easy. I move towards bliss every time.

This past year my theme has been simplicity. Going through a divorce and splitting belongings taught me that stuff means nothing. Yet, when I begin to have too much stuff, I feel my stress level increasing in relation to how much stuff I have. I am constantly cycling through purging and donating items for others to use. I am always purging. Taking a run to the local landfill or the local thrift shop to donate clothing my family no longer uses gives me so much energy it is almost silly. Who would have thought giving away your stuff would make you feel better.

Beyond the physical environment, I also try to keep things simple in my life by living clean and light. Just like eating clean, living clean means you keep the noise and distraction out of your life as much as possible. This doesn't mean I am not busy, it means I control my schedule and I stay aware and realistic about how I schedule my days. I do my best not to overcommit. I allow for a buffer for meetings to go a bit longer than expected so I am not running behind. I remind myself to collect memories and experiences rather than things. I sort through my clothes to keep the items I love so even getting dressed is easier (and so that my clean laundry has a place to be put away). And yes, some days my house looks like it blew up, but it never stays that way.

I make a conscious effort to draw joy from the simple things in life: the fresh spring rain, warm sun on my face, a cup of creamy coffee, a summer walk, or a sweet kiss.

Can you think of any possible simplicity routines that you could integrate into your life to give you a moment to regularly help you slow down to savor the abundance that is actually all around you? (This fall, regular teatime with my sister hits my list! I also need to catch up with my friend Tisha over what may end up being several pieces of her famous d'Lish by Tish Wacky Chocolate Cake.)

Chapter 19:
SURROUND AND SUBMERSE YOURSELF

When I first separated I was desperately seeking happiness. I didn't know where to look for it, what it might look like, or how to bring it into my life. So I painted my walls and added colour into my life. I started listening to music to fill the silence in my home when the kids were not with me. I even stenciled this quote above my bed,

"If you want to be happy, be." ~ Leo Tolstoy

Every single day I looked at that quote and wondered if that was the secret to happiness. I questioned what "be" actually meant. Did it mean be you, be still, or be whatever you want?

As confused as I was, every single time I walked into my room, I saw this happiness quote and was reminded about my desire to move towards happiness. I was training myself to look for happiness. It stayed on my mind because I was reminded of my desire daily.

Likewise, when I first started my journey to increase my fitness, I converted a room in the basement to my home gym and stenciled "Wish It... Dream It...Do It!" on the ledge of a dropped ceiling so that when I was on the workout bench I would see the words. I had nothing else to look at but the words. I dropped twenty pounds in twelve weeks.

My bed has a toss cushion that reads, "to the moon and back," a saying that I share with my children when I tell them I love them. On the stove burns a candle that says, "Choose Happiness." When I drink my coffee, it is out of a mug saturated with positive words, phrases and action statements. I have positive life manifestos in huge canvases on my wall. My computer has motivational screen savers. I wear bracelets that drip in positive words – believe, love, faith and hope. I have vision boards and frames in a few places, and I use my passwords as therapy!

Password therapy? Let me explain. Have you ever stopped to count how many times in a day you have to type in a password to access your phone or computer? I make all my passwords phrases that keep me focused on my goals. For example, when I was working on my self-esteem, "urenuff" served as a constant reminder that I didn't need to be better or different – just true to myself. I typed that message thirty times a day at least. Guess what I began to believe? I am enough.

When I had created some financial goals, I used the goal number as my password to keep me aware that I was saving money and to avoid slipping into default spending habits. Other times I used theme words like bliss or simplicity and a number that signifies how long I will focus on that goal. What "password therapy" does is serve as a constant, gentle reminder I have things I wish to work towards and by staying aware of this, I make better choices, which in turn, brings about better results. The password can snap me back on track and increase my awareness just like that!

I surround myself with positivity. Do you? If you don't, can you think of ways some of these things might work for you?

Chapter 20:
BE SOCIAL

Make time for friends and build healthy relationships. If you are struggling and that involves pulling away and isolating yourself, try really hard to extend yourself and connect with your social network. If your social network is strong and nourished it will be there when the chips are down. If you have a social network that is not supportive of your desires and causes distractions as you strive towards happiness, develop and nurture a new one.

෨∽෨

"When top scientists and psychologists talk about what's important to our overall well-being and how satisfied we are with our lives, the only thing that they all agree on is that social relationships are probably the single best predictor of our overall happiness." ~Tom Rath

෨∽෨

Whom you associate with matters. I have heard that you are most like the five people you spend your time with. What does that mean for you? Will these people help you move towards bliss or will their bad habits lure you into a stagnant pool of despair over time? Humans are capable of amazing transformation, but to move from one place to another, you need everyone (friends, environment, and mindset) all pushing in the same direction.

If we make our choices from what is presented in our environment, it makes sense to clean it up as much as we can – friends, habits, and any other factors that will either support us or pull us down. Does the world shape us or do we shape the world? Consider you social network. YOU have some say as to whom you let into your exclusive circle. You are in control of that. Once these people are in your social network, they begin to influence and shape you. So ultimately, it all becomes a matter of your initial choice. **Keep the circle tight and clean.**

I remember reading somewhere that change is hard and we have so many things working against us that make change even more difficult for us to achieve or to maintain long-term. In fact, Jonathan Haidt says change can only remain sustainable if one of two things happens: **there must be a change in the environment or your relationships.** Change won't last if your relationships or environment stays the same. This is why community is vital. If you want to change yourself, change your peer group, and change your environment.

If you get this one right, a SHIFT, rather than the shit, will hit the fan!

Chapter 21:
BE STILL

We multi-task all day long. Phones ring and beep for our attention. We open our web browser and are flooded with images that entice us and do all they can to derail our focus. We talk on the phone while typing or cleaning out our junk drawer. We cook supper and catch up with busy kids who have one foot in the front door and the other out the back. We read lost school newsletters and realize we need a dozen cupcakes for tomorrow's bake sale. Then, we drop the f-bomb because there isn't enough time in the day to stay on top of it all.

Become still. Refuel. Rest.

Rest is so important but it is often overlooked. Research consistently links decreased sleep to decreased happiness. I don't know about you but I can wake up a different person if I am sleep-deprived. My ex-husband didn't call me "swamp monster" for no reason. Lack of sleep truly does impair our cognitive functioning. I am sure you are all familiar with the tests done on drunk drivers and sleep deprived drivers. Discovery Channel's investigation, *Driving Tired*, clearly established that driving tired equals driving impaired. If that is so, what does lack of sleep do to your other brain functions? Lack of sleep not only messes with your mood, but it impacts your memory and your immune system as well. I know when I am sleep deprived, challenges I would ordinarily take in stride can bring me to my knees. Coping mechanisms crumble and stress levels soar! Sleep deprivation will not put you in your happy place. You certainly won't get there any faster by taking this common, socially accepted "shortcut" that actually takes you further away from what you crave.

Many people are not even aware of how chronically sleep-deprived they are. When I feel my life starting to tank, I institute the nighttime alarm ritual. I set my phone alarm to go off at ten p.m. every night, at which time I brush my teeth and crawl into bed. I set my morning alarm to go off seven or eight hours later. Within a few nights of this practice, I feel substantially better. I am sharper mentally and more productive. I begin to wake up without my alarm. Everything seems easier. Problems seem more manageable. I get more done in less time and feel way better. Plus, I know that adequate sleep helps my hormones to regulate which helps me maintain my weight. If I start to puff up I examine my sleeping habits.

How is your sleep? Do you get seven to eight hours a night? Do you use your phone or computer prior to going to bed or do you fall asleep watching TV? Do you use sleep aids? Do you have a relaxing ritual for going to bed that helps you unwind?

If you need to sleep in until two p.m. on weekends to catch up, something is lacking in your sleeping patterns. Ultimately your goal is to have a regular pattern that has you up every day at the same time, with no catch-ups required.

Rest. Refuel.

Chapter 22:
ANTICIPATE GOODNESS

I can't leave this one out.

Actually, the more I think of the impact of this one on your mental health, the more excited I get. Anticipate goodness. Please make sure you savor that one.

Anticipate goodness. Expect it. Look for it.

Look forward to the wonderful things coming your way. Use your dreams and desires to give yourself something magnificent to look forward to but understand, in most cases, all this goodness will not arrive on its own.

This is where you step in to act. Plot. Create. Scheme. Whip up wonderful things with your BFFs over a bottle of wine. Plan that trip to the lake for the last weekend of summer and then look forward to it all summer long with anticipation of how amazing it will be to close your summer off with such blissful memories. Plan to do the things you know you will enjoy. Pick out a special book to read that weekend or a meal to prepare and enjoy with friends. Have backup plans for rainy days too (or snowy ones) so that you don't see them as a roadblock or a wasted day. For example, I love summer and look forward to the loosely planned outings I have on my list of things to do like hitting the local lake with my daughter and our kayaks or the annual camping trip with our friends.

If plans go awry because I wake up and it's raining, I make sure I have a solid plan B. There are always things to do. Perhaps I declare the first rain day garage-cleaning day. It has to get done regardless, and why waste a sunny day later in the year? That sure beats sitting inside stewing over the fact that my initial plans didn't work out. I never feel like I am wasting time.

Before I hear you say, "but I don't have a lake to go to," or "I have no money to make plans" this is about doing something YOU will anticipate and something within your means. Maybe it is a one-hour massage at the end of your busiest season at work. Maybe it is finally arranging and sticking to that coffee or lunch date with a friend you love but never get to see anymore. Commit to something so you can savor the anticipation of the event. Anticipating the event allows you to feel excited and shifts your focus to what you look forward to.

I love to travel. I try to book a few trips a year when I am able to get away. I anticipate the new experiences or the down time I think will come with the trips I take. If it is a beach vacation in the middle of the Canadian winter, I anticipate the relaxing mornings with coffee in hand, the sun on my face, the sand between my toes, the smell of the ocean, and the freedom to sleep in a bit (even though I never do because I can't wait to get up and make the most of the day, but at least I have the choice.)

I usually book my winter vacations in the fall and then I have four to five months to anticipate the joy I will have on the trip. Much like recording and reflecting, this allows me to get more bang for my buck! Mentally, I can take that trip a million times in my head and it brings me some joy, especially when the cold of winter has descended on me and I lack motivation and feel like the winter will never end. I get to enjoy that anticipation of getting off of that plane and being engulfed in one big humid hug.

Anticipation can be more exciting than the actual kiss. But the kiss can kick ass too!

PART 4:
Information to Transformation

We all have a story. We have watched our personal stories play out as we have moved through life, and up until this point you may have never considered that YOU are also the one who has the power and responsibility to create your story to be anything you want it to be.

"WOW," you might be thinking, this is surely overkill. Does she really do all these things to be happy on purpose? Truth be told, no I do not do ALL of these things at once but the more of them I do, the more successful I am at maintaining the happiness mindset and changing my behaviors. Each of the elements keeps me alert and focused on my goal of happiness. Having all these tools (and many more) in my back pocket allows me to flirt with life and enjoy my journey. The bottom line is I have spent a considerable amount of time being unhappy and now I just want to blow the lid off my life and live it big.

The best analogy I have ever heard about creating sustainable change in one's life compares making change to pushing a car out of snow bank. I alluded to this earlier when I talked about social connections but let me explain it a bit further. In *Change Anything: The New Science of Personal Success*, the authors suggest if you have six people willing to push the car out, you will have greater success if all the people are pushing in the same direction. (Duh?) It isn't going to work out so well if three people are pushing from the front of the car and three from the back.

This analogy stuck with me because I tend to think in pictures and I live in Canada where pushing cars is common practice... it makes complete sense to me. Now, take this analogy and apply it to your own life! When I did this, I was surprised to find a few circumstances where I had five people pushing from the front while I pushed alone from the back! No wonder it seemed like I was struggling, I WAS!

Now when I find myself struggling, I picture the *issue* as a car and look to see where my pushers are placed. It can clear up some situations pretty quickly and gives me a solid action plan for making things easier. If you feel like you are wading in quicksand as you try to make change, set yourself up for success by placing all six "people" behind the car. ("People" can be real people in your life, happiness habits or external variables.) *Practice gratitude* to shift your focus. *Record and reflect* positive events that happen in your life so you get to enjoy them more than once. *Change relationships and your environment* so you are supported. *Plan and book things* that excite you so that you can benefit from the anticipation of the event as well as the event itself. Some years the ONLY thing getting me through a long, cold, Canadian winter is the anticipation of a trip to Mexico. If I book that holiday in November and I don't go anywhere until February, I get to anticipate that trip for months before I go and as such, the anticipation creates a physical reaction in my body and mind.

If you don't believe me, think way back to the anticipation you felt about a first date or a first kiss with someone you were totally crazy about. Or, daydream right now about your secret crush or your sexy spouse grabbing you and kissing you madly.

Now look me straight in the eyes and tell me that the anticipation of such an event didn't move you.

I saw you squirm.

Stop smiling.

No, I mean it. Why are you grinning like that? You looked flushed.

See my point?

Surround yourself with reminders of what is important to you and put your environment to work for you. There is a reason your mother didn't like those friends of yours back in the day; she saw their influence on you! Who is in your social circle now? Are they helping or hindering you? *Get social* with people whom you admire and who possess the traits and characteristics you desire. Connect with these people. *Practice kindness* every chance you get and make it fun! Smile at people and make eye contact, open doors, buy the coffee of the person behind you in that lazy Tim Horton's line. Not only does it snap the recipient out of their train of thought, "Oh wow! Someone bought me a coffee," but you feel pretty sneaky doing it and driving away to leave them to figure out why!

Finally, I leave you with this.
We all have a story. We get to decide who the main characters will be, their disposition, and their role in the story line. We also have some control over who leaves our story and when. While we may not always have control over the circumstances

our characters face, we do have control over how they react to what happens. We get to determine the choices they make. If at any time, you do not like how your story is being played out, YOU CAN CHANGE IT.

The only question that remains now is... WILL YOU?
Now you have some solid happy tactics to implement in to your life. If you are interested in knowing more, there are many great books on positive psychology and the science of happiness that can bury you in strategies you can apply to increase your happiness. However, sometimes more is not better. You have enough here to make substantial change in your life. You don't need more ideas. You need movement. You need action. You need momentum. You can get more ideas when you have begun sorting, applying and tweaking the ones here.

Action is what it is all about now. If you do nothing with all I have shared with you, nothing will change. Life, as you know it, will remain the same. You will wake up tomorrow and do exactly what you did today. You will think the same way about the same things (causing the same behaviors). You will behave the same way because we are creatures of habit and habit is a default behavior. You will have the same results because nothing will have changed.

But, I know that's not why you are here. You came here to get *Happy on Purpose*. Doing so, requires an action and you have what you need to get started. Accept responsibility and get creative.

Your life is waiting for you. Live it big.

Find Your Way

There are so many ways to create happiness in your life that to limit it to my suggestions alone would fall short of serving you. I didn't want to overwhelm you but I wanted you to know your options are endless, so I asked Mary Sabo to share her top ten tips for cultivating happiness with us.

1. Accept yourself in the here and now.
    a. Understand that you are exactly where you're supposed to be. You are at a specific part of your own unique journey and allowing yourself to accept that creates a foundation for you to start building your happiest life.
    b. "And so rock bottom became the solid foundation on which I rebuilt my life." – J.K. Rowling
2. Rediscover your child-like imagination and passion.
    a. Before we knew we had limits – we dreamt without judgment. Explore your old hobbies, whip out your magic cape, tune your dusty guitar and remember just because we're grown up, we're not devoid of dreams and passion. Realize just because you didn't end up heading to the Olympics, win a Grammy or star on Broadway – it doesn't mean these passions shouldn't be part of your life.
3. Inventory and release resentments.
    a. When we harbor resentments against another– we keep ourselves attached to them. We actively allow them to rent space in our head and let our ego go to

town. Identify your resentments, find your part in it and then let go. Taking responsibility allows you to actually let go and move forward freely.

4. First things first.

    a. Any creative person will tell you that many times they don't have any issue visualizing their big picture but struggle with actually getting the concept off the ground. Before you overwhelm yourself with the size of your vision and logistics, remember to put first things first. You can't worry about what teaching hospital you'll get picked for residency if you haven't found out the proper steps to get into Medical School in the first place.

5. Allow yourself to come undone.

    a. There is one moment, after all the immediate chaos of 9/11 diminished and a black cloud rolled through my town with funeral after funeral that I found a pearl of wisdom in an ocean of tragedy. My mother told her friend, the woman who had just lost her husband and was ever strong, that it was OK to cry and it was OK to not be OK. The woman buckled and sobbed. No one else had taken the time to really let her not be OK – which is what she needed. We need to let go of the antiquated idea that when something shitty happens we should hide our feelings in order to heal.

6. Remember, the morning always comes.

    a. "It's always darkest before the dawn." (Florence and the Machine, *Shake It Out*) Remember the quote "In the middle of the pain, lies the existence of opportunity." Take your dark nights and shine light on them in a way that moves you forward and allows for a positive outlook. Life is unpredictable; there will be times of great happiness but also times when it feels like the floor falls out beneath us. Have faith and continue to march on. You never know, your story may inspire another who goes through something similar after you.

7. Foster relationships.
    a. Nothing is permanent. Life begins and ends. Fortunes are made and lost. Beauty comes and fades. We are meant to connect with others. Remember the value of a good friend or loved one and the prescription for almost anything: shared memories and a great belly laugh.

8. Remain Teachable.
    a. The minute you decide you know it all, you lose the ability to grow and thrive. Humility allows us to relate to others as well as ourselves. History shows the greatest figures and influential individuals are the ones who continue to explore and question what they don't know.

9. Keep it simple and be grateful.
    a. What is it we really need to make us happy? A closet stacked with shoes? A loaded bank account? A full date book? When we place our happiness on external things we are always going to be left wanting more, more shoes once ours go out of style, more money once it's been spent, more events once the foods been eaten and the last guest goes home. Keep it simple and express gratitude – that you have a pair of shoes to wear, that you have money to put

food on the table and that you have one or two close friends to share secrets, sorrow and joy with.

10. You can always start your day over.

    a.   Sometimes, no matter how hard we try, some days will just suck. You have the option, at any time, to wipe the slate and start the day over.

Mary Sabo is a Long Island native who grew up with dreams of lighting up the Broadway stage. Depression and anxiety coupled with self-destructive behaviors led her to hit a severe emotional and physical bottom at the young age of 23. After a time of self-searching and picking up the pieces she realized happiness was not something she'd find outside herself. Her need for the spotlight transformed into a driving desire to help others find lasting happiness as she had. You can find her at www.Mary-Sabo.com.

Acknowledgements

I have so many people cheering me on and I couldn't possibly list everyone here, but please know I appreciate your support and love. It doesn't go unnoticed and it is likely on my gratitude list! If you taught me a hard lesson, I really do thank you for it. Life is just so damn amazing and unpredictable. Thanks for the love, the laughter, and the lessons and for believing in me.

Thank you to Cara Loper of Loose Lid Creative for always designing covers that speak to my message. Also, thank you for the story you shared in this book. Your heart makes this world a better place, and your creativity makes for awesome book covers! Angelique Trigueros, you are quite possibly the most hilarious person I know. Your contribution to this book and your feedback is most appreciated and I know we will remain friends for our lifetime. Mary Sabo, thank you for being open to sharing your wisdom with the world. I love your message and I look forward to watching the ripple! Karen Cooke–Grant, I hate that we live so far away but this friendship never wanes. When I think of how it began, I smile every time. Pneumonia, yeah right!

To my editors Cara Lockwood, Shelly Drymon, and Beth Jarrell thank you for the extra set of eyes and the many suggestion to strengthen this book into a useful happiness guide for others.

Finally, to my family, I can't express the gratitude I have for being part of the Sparks clan. Open minded, loving, creative thinkers are all around me. Alex and Chiara, thank you for all you do to make me a better mother and human and for all the support, love, and awesome laughs. I am not sure how I raised such amazing children! Mom, Dad, Terri and Larry, thank you for reality checks, support, and the witty comments that keep it all real. I am truly blessed... like, to the moon and back blessed. True, true ... you have to cherish what you have and focus on those things. May your path be blessed and filled with bliss. Always. And I hope I am at your side.

Freebies & Additional Resources

Thanks for reading! If you have enjoyed what I shared with you, then please take a moment to check out some ways you can get more of my content for free. And, if I may be so bold, please leave a review on Amazon so other readers know what to expect.

Grab your **FREE Life Assessment Tool** from my website (www.swiftkicklife.com.)

Listen in on the **GET HAPPY NOW Radio Show** with Jennifer Sparks on the True2YouRadio Network (www. True2YouRadio.com.)

Grab a FREE chapter from my first book, **WTF to OMG: The Frazzled Female's Guide to Creating a Life You Love.** _You can take a peek inside my book on Amazon. com, but you have to download the free chapter from my website._

If you are interested in grabbing a printed copy of WTF to OMG, use code: **7AN3LA6A** at this link (https://www. createspace.com/4397328) to save 25% off the retail price.

Note: While I cannot promise how long the coupon code will be valid, I did want to reward your interest and loyalty and this is the only way, at this time, I know how!

Furthermore, *WTF to OMG* has been purchased in duplicate copy by many women for gifts for friends. I have NO objection if you use this code to purchase multiple copies at a 25% discount.

If you are interested in learning more about what I can do to help you transform your life, please visit www.swiftkicklife.com. You can find information about one-on-one coaching programs, online courses and face-to-face events. I come to serve you from the place of having been there. I would love to help you create that kick ass, amazing life you dream of living!

Connect with me on social media and let's start talking!
Facebook: www.Facebook.com/swiftkickfitness
Twitter: www.twitter.com/swiftkickfitnes
Instagram: www.instagram.com/swiftkickfit